# CONTENTS

# THE REIGN OF THE DINOSAURS

Jean-Guy Michard

THAMES AND HUDSON

Far from being the 'failure of evolution' we used to read about in natural-science textbooks, dinosaurs marked a wonderful stage of life on earth. Spread throughout the world – fossilized remains have been unearthed in Europe, Asia, Africa, North and South America, Antarctica and Australia – there were approximately thirty families of dinosaurs. We have much to learn about these extinct reptiles, and we must dispel some of the misconceptions.

## CHAPTER 1
## IN PRAISE OF DIVERSITY

Bringing dinosaurs back from the dead requires a thorough knowledge of their anatomy. It can also lead to daring speculation, such as that involving this *Stenonychosaurus* and 'dinosauroid' pair (right).

Dinosaurs enjoy a place of honour in prehistory. They died out millions of years ago; yet their hold on the imagination of children and, less consciously, of grown-ups is as powerful as ever. But few still think of them in terms of the archetypal Dinosaur, that grotesque, forbidding monster whose stupidity was matched only by its 'inordinate' size. On the contrary, the hundreds of currently known species fascinate laypeople and specialists alike precisely because these creatures developed such a wide range of forms and adaptations throughout the Mesozoic era (approximately 215 to 65 million years ago).

The first specimen of *Compsognathus* was discovered in 1861 in lithographic limestone quarries near Kelheim, Germany. The fine-grained sediment kept it remarkably well preserved.

## The surprising variety of dinosaurs

Dinosaurs may have been the biggest animals ever to walk the earth, but not all of them were giants. One small, bipedal Late Jurassic dinosaur, *Compsognathus*, was no bigger than a rooster. This diminutive carnivore weighed just a few kilos and measured ninety cm at most from the tip of its snout to the end of its extremely long tail. At the opposite pole, bulky quadrupedal herbivores like *Brachiosaurus* (twenty-five metres long, sixty metric tons) come closer to what people picture as the classic dinosaur. But even this heavyweight has been outclassed. Discovered in 1972 and 1979 respectively, *Supersaurus* and, above all, *Ultrasaurus* smashed all records for sheer size. Although the identification of *Ultrasaurus* was based mostly on a shoulder blade, this creature probably measured more than thirty metres in length and weighed an estimated 135 tons – earthshaking and mind-boggling figures when you stop and think that the average full-grown elephant weighs a mere five tons!

Between these two extremes, dinosaurs ran an incredible morphological gamut, from nimble two-footed running carnivores and herbivores weighing less than one hundred kilos to multi-ton titans plodding about on all fours, some whose bodies bristled with bony spikes, others whose heads were studded with fearsome horns. This succession of forms spanned virtually the whole of the Mesozoic era, from the Triassic, through the Jurassic, and on into the Cretaceous period.

Adapting in highly varied ways to the stresses of their environment, the last dinosaurs were poles apart

In 1866 Edward Drinker Cope named the small carnivorous dinosaur on the left in this old illustration *Laelaps*, but in 1877 fellow American Othniel Charles Marsh, another palaeontologist, changed it to *Dryptosaurus*, because *Laelaps* had already been assigned to an insect. At any rate, it is hard to believe that a single one of these creatures could inflict much harm on a giant like *Apatosaurus* (the correct scientific name of *Brontosaurus*).

from the first. The oldest dinosaur fossils date from
the Late Triassic, about 200
million years ago. These remains are
so scarce and fragmentary that
scientists have not yet been able
to pinpoint the exact origin
of the two main groups
living at the time, the
prosauropods and the small carnivorous
dinosaurs collectively known as coelurosaurs. The
prosauropods died out early on, at the dawn of the
Jurassic, probably swept aside by the explosion of
life-forms that occurred during this period. Certain
groups, such as                    hadrosaurs and

ceratopsians, did not appear until the middle of the following geological period, the Cretaceous. As is the case since the beginning of life on earth, newcomers filled the ecological niches of those that died out.

Thus, dinosaurs did not constitute an undifferentiated zoological group, but a radiating succession of families, each with its own successive genera and species, each destined to meet its particular fate. Nevertheless, when the Cretaceous drew to a close 64.5 million years ago, the creatures that so richly deserve to be called the Monarchs of the Mesozoic became totally extinct.

A natomists quickly learned to distinguish pterosaur fossils from those of other reptiles and birds.

## Mesozoic animal life is abundant and diversified, but the reptiles are its undisputed masters

Dinosaurs may have reigned supreme during the Mesozoic, but they were far from alone. They shared their realm with many other land-dwelling reptiles, some of whom have remarkably similar-looking present-day counterparts (tortoises and crocodiles, for example). Conversely, the sole surviving descendant of the rhynchocephalids, a group of reptiles that flourished for about 100 million years from the Triassic to the Cretaceous, is the tuatara, a lizard whose range is now limited to a few small islands in New Zealand.

The skies and seas of Mesozoic times were not devoid of life, either. Pterosaurs, often lumped together with dinosaurs, marked the first attempt on the part of vertebrates to colonize the air.

I n this painting by Charles R. Knight (left), three very different zoological groups can be spotted among the predominant cycads of a Late Jurassic landscape: dinosaurs, represented by the small theropod *Compsognathus*; birds, represented by the oldest-known specimen, *Archaeopteryx*; and flying reptiles, represented by *Rhamphorhynchus*.

Set in Early Cretaceous Australia, this painting by Mark Hallett features a few of the major dinosaur groups. In the foreground a small *Fulgurotherium* and, to the right, two *Muttaburrasaurus* represent bipedal herbivores. Behind them, to the left, three ankylosaurs (armoured dinosaurs) known as *Minmi*, together with the bulky long-necked sauropods in the background, are examples of herbivorous quadrupeds. Two carnivores with sharp claws and pointed teeth round out the picture: the carnosaur *Rapator*, attempting to feed while warding off an intrusive pair of flying reptiles; and the far more agile coelurosaur *Kakuru* (left foreground).

Various groups of marine reptiles plied the Mesozoic waters: streamlined ichthyosaurs; plesiosaurs, which looked like barrel-bodied snakes; and mosasaurs, with their forbidding jaws, which actually were nothing more than gigantic lizards adapted to living in water.

The rich and varied fauna of this era also included insects, crustaceans, fish, amphibians – and mammals, mouse-sized creatures skulking about in the shadow of the dinosaurs and awaiting their moment of glory.

### Try to picture a human being not as a mammal, but as a descendant of the dinosaurs

If dinosaurs are the stock-in-trade of science-fiction writers, things take on an altogether different complexion when scientists become involved. How might dinosaurs have evolved had they not vanished forever from the face of the earth 64.5 million years ago?

In 1982 Canadian palaeontologist Dale A. Russell

The marine reptiles of Mesozoic times, such as ichthyosaurs and plesiosaurs, were very often considered to be dinosaurs. However, palaeontologists quickly learned to tell them apart by their distinctive anatomical features. Clashes between ichthyosaurs and plesiosaurs were a favourite subject of illustrators during the 19th and early 20th centuries. Endowed with more or less fictitious attributes – crested backs, forked tongues, bulging eyes – these adversaries created an impression of cruelty and ferociousness that seemed appropriate for prehistoric monsters.

carried out an intriguing 'thought experiment', to use Russell's own words. As a starting point he selected the reconstructions of the *Stenonychosaurus*, a small carnivorous dinosaur discovered in Late Cretaceous Alberta. This animal already boasted a set of highly advanced characteristics: a large brain, stereoscopic vision resulting from partially overlapping visual fields, a bipedal gait and prehensile hands.

By extrapolating its evolution until its ratio of brain weight to body weight was comparable to that of *Homo sapiens*, the researcher came up with – and constructed a model of – a so-called dinosauroid. If this hypothetical creature had actually evolved, it could have competed with humans. Fortunately or unfortunately, however, more than sixty million years separate the last dinosaur from the first human being.

A visitor from the depths of time, the tuatara, whose ancestors lived alongside the dinosaurs, is now on the road to extinction. Confined to the small islands in Cook Strait, New Zealand, this relict species lives in burrows and feeds on small invertebrates.

The eerie gaze of the dinosauroid's reptilian eyes seems to mirror our own questionings about the vagaries of evolution. Appearances notwithstanding, this wholly hypothetical dinosaur-human resulted from a combination of scientific reasoning – carried to extremes, to be sure – and an undeniable flair for creative thought: proof that, in palaeontology, the rational and the fanciful can go hand in hand.

People have always been intrigued by unusually shaped rocks, and interest in fossil bones and shells has been documented since ancient Greek times. The possibility that these petrified formations might have had an organic source was ruled out, clearing the way for all sorts of hypotheses. 'The earth brings forth bones and… bone-like rocks,' wrote Theophrastus of Lesbos (372–287 BC).

## CHAPTER 2
# IN SEARCH OF AN IDENTITY

To reconstruct a dinosaur like *Iguanodon* (left) successfully, one must first know how to decipher the record in the rocks. Seeking and unearthing the remains of these gigantic reptiles is just one facet of palaeontologists' work. Their chief mission is to understand what sort of creatures dinosaurs were.

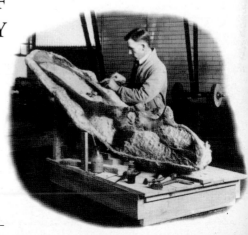

For centuries strongly held religious beliefs made it impossible to come up with a coherent scientific view of the world before the emergence of humans. To preserve the established order of creation, any fossil bones were for a long time dismissed as freaks of nature. Dinosaurs were no exception to the rule.

## The first mention of what is probably a dinosaur bone does not appear until the end of the 17th century

In 1677 English naturalist Robert Plot described and illustrated in his *Natural History of Oxford-Shire* what he identified with remarkable accuracy as the lower end of a large fossilized femur. At first Plot thought it might be an elephant bone, but then he concluded that it belonged to a giant human. In 1763 R. Brookes concurred and, using the zoological nomenclature Linnaeus had devised a few years earlier, assigned the piece a scientific name based on its pendulous shape: *Scrotum humanum.*

Five years later Jean-François Robinet, a Frenchman of the Enlightenment whose scientific thinking sparked considerable controversy, theorized that this

In every civilization, dragons, monsters, chimeras and other mythical creatures have haunted human imagination. By the 17th century, however, even the great winged, fire-spitting dragons of Europe, bristling with claws and spikes, could not hold out against the advance of science. They gave way to the less terrifying, more 'plausible' composites described in explorers' accounts, such as the creatures Antonio Tempesta depicted in 1636 (below). It was many years before real-life dragons, the dinosaurs, were found, but even the most nightmarish mythologies could not rival them for sheer variety.

bone fragment was an actual petrified scrotum – evidence of nature's successive attempts at perfecting an 'ideal human type'. Sadly, the fossil in question no longer exists; but it probably came from a large carnivorous dinosaur of the family Megalosauridae. The fact that the fragment was not correctly identified until two centuries after its discovery indicates just how slowly science progressed.

## The dinosaurs of Normandy

As early as the second half of the 18th century, people were travelling far and wide in search of dinosaur fossils. Some came to Normandy, in western France, where certain geological strata exposed during low tide turned up intriguing petrified material. One naturalist from Le Havre, Abbé Jacques-François Dicquemare, did more than seek, find and collect. He understood. 'I had little difficulty noticing that the material sheathing each piece differed from that at the centre. I made out what appeared to be bone….'

In 1776, when Dicquemare described his fossils in the *Journal de Physique*, he took what was in those days a strictly scientific stance and refrained from speculating on their possible source. Although most of

When Robert Plot's book was published, the very concept of dinosaurs did not yet exist. Large fossil bones, if not thought to be the remains of giant humans, were seldom described accurately.

them came from other reptiles –
crocodiles, plesiosaurs and ichthyosaurs –
one large, meticulously described femur
seems to have belonged to a dinosaur.

Another Frenchman, Georges Cuvier,
visited Normandy between 1788 and
1795. He had not yet turned his attention
to fossil vertebrates and did not collect
any at the time. The Mesozoic reptile vertebrae he
mentioned in a scientific article of 1800 had, in fact,
been culled from the Honfleur region of France by
clergyman-naturalist Abbé Bachelet of Rouen, whose
collection was transferred to the Museum of Natural
History in Paris after his death. In
1808 Cuvier published illustrations
of these vertebrae and assigned
them to two different unknown
species of crocodile, adding

The cliffs of
Normandy rank
among the shrines of
French palaeontology.
The remains of Late
Jurassic vertebrates
abound at the bottom of
these chalk formations,
but nowadays silting
makes it impossible to
reach fossil-bearing strata
most of the time.
Scientists and laypeople
still flock here in hopes of
finding fossil bones, but
only during those few
hours a year when tides
are abnormally low.

that some of the pieces had rather peculiar anatomical characteristics. While some of the fossils did indeed come from a crocodile, Cuvier had also just described and drawn the remains of a carnivorous dinosaur, though he was not yet aware of it.

Bones have undoubtedly been unearthed in North America for a very long time, but the earliest reliable written accounts date from the late 18th century. In 1787 Caspar Wistar and Timothy Matlack informed the American Philosophical Society of Philadelphia that they had discovered a 'giant's bone' in New Jersey. And in 1806, while exploring the upper course of the Missouri River, William Clark mentioned in his expedition diary that a gigantic 'fish rib' had been found partially embedded in a bluff along the Yellowstone River in Montana.

Giants or fish? Judging by their size and provenance, the bones from New Jersey and Montana probably belonged to dinosaurs. In fact, these very regions are now famous for the Mesozoic reptile remains they have been yielding for well over a century.

### A dinosaur is named and described for the first time: *Megalosaurus*, the 'great lizard'

This word was coined in 1822 by James Parkinson, who, though he correctly identified the nervous disorder that bears his name, published the term *Megalosaurus* without describing the material on which he based the new genus. Consequently, *Megalosaurus* was not considered a bona-fide scientific entity until two years later, when William Buckland, of Oxford University, published a detailed description

Georges Cuvier noted the similarity between the remains of England's *Megalosaurus* and the vertebrae from France in 1824, but not before travelling to England to meet with William Buckland a second time (1818). In 1832 Hermann von Meyer assigned them the name *Streptospondylus*.

of fossil bones he had been collecting for some years at Stonesfield, near Oxford. Buckland correctly attributed these remains to a gigantic carnivorous reptile that had no known equivalent in modern nature, and the 'great lizard' took its place on the stage of palaeontology. This first dinosaur soon had company, for just then – again in England – another equally strange reptile was coming back from the dead.

## Gideon Mantell, *Iguanodon*, and the question of Cuvier's alleged 'diagnosis'

Gideon Mantell was a country doctor from Sussex who happened to have a passion for fossils. It is said that in 1822, while he was visiting a patient, his wife, Mary Ann, stayed outdoors and chanced upon a peculiar-looking tooth in a pile of broken stone used for repairing roads. Mantell believed it to be a very old fossilized tooth even though it bore no apparent resemblance to any known tooth. It was rather worn and sparked little enthusiasm among specialists who examined it. Other specimens had to be found. Fortunately, Mantell had become quite familiar with the area while making his rounds and managed to locate the sediment that had contained the specimen. He paid quarrymen working in Tilgate Forest to look for fossils, and in the summer of 1822 they provided him with additional teeth.

The earliest pictures of *Iguanodon* and *Megalosaurus* (right) are quite different from present-day reconstructions. The skeletal anatomy of the extinct reptiles was not fully understood at the time and was therefore modelled after that of reptiles living today. *Iguanodon* looks like an oversized iguana; *Megalosaurus*, like a huge monitor lizard.

"With the teeth constructed so as to cut with the whole of their concave edge, each movement of the jaws produced the combined effect of a knife and a saw, at the same time that the point made a first incision like that made by the point of a double-cutting sword. The backward curvature taken by the teeth at their full growth rendered the escape of the prey when once seized impossible.... We find here, then, the same arrangements which enabled mankind to put in operation many of the instruments which they employ."
William Buckland, quoted in Louis Figuier's *The World Before the Deluge*, 1874

The distinguished British scientists of the Geological Society of London persisted in their belief that his fossils came from a recent fish or mammal. But Mantell was equally persistent. He sent his finds to Georges Cuvier, with whom he had been corresponding since 1821. Some maintain that the great French anatomist 'diagnosed' a rhinoceros. In point of fact, what he did was to theorize that the fossils belonged to a large unknown herbivorous reptile.

At long last, a fossil hunter named Samuel Stutchbury found the clue to the puzzle. He said the teeth that had given Mantell so much difficulty looked exactly like iguana teeth, only bigger. They did belong to a fossilized reptile after all.

Thus, in 1825, *Iguanodon* became the second dinosaur to be given a scientific name. However, its pointed thumb bone was mistaken for a horn and placed on top of its snout, vitiating attempts at an accurate physical description.

To counter the scepticism surrounding *Iguanodon*'s name and classification as a reptile, Gideon Mantell published a plate with illustrations of modern iguana teeth alongside the fossilized teeth he had been collecting since 1822.

WEALDEN FORMATION. 1 & 2. IGUANODON. 3. HYLAEOSAURU

Gideon Mantell's drawing of an *Iguanodon* (right).

## 'Altogether peculiar reptiles': the creation of a distinct zoological group

Sixteen years after the description of *Iguanodon*, nine genera of large land-dwelling Mesozoic reptiles had been identified and given scientific names. They were overgrown reptiles, to be sure, but reptiles just the same and deserving of a zoological category all their own. At least, that is what occurred to Richard Owen as he reexamined the fossil reptiles of the British Isles. An astute anatomist, Owen realized that, for all their similarities to present-day reptiles, these extinct creatures also had quite a few features that set them apart from living counterparts. In 1841, at the annual meeting of the British Association for the

What greater spectacle could the general public of the mid-1800s hope to behold than dinosaurs and other prehistoric beasts rising from the dead, if not in flesh and blood, then as lifesize reconstructions? So Richard Owen must have argued when he told sculptor and painter Benjamin Waterhouse Hawkins of his plans. Under Owen's scientific supervision, tons of brick, cement, wood and iron scrap were assembled into sculptures in Hawkins' studio. (Left: an etching of two of the sculptures.) To celebrate their completion, Owen invited twenty dignitaries to a private viewing on 31 December 1853. It was novel, to say the least. Guests at the dinner party were seated around a table laid out in the belly of an *Iguanodon*. The site chosen for the exhibition was the same park just outside London in which the huge Crystal Palace was re-erected by order of Queen Victoria. Its effect on the public was tremendous. Although these reconstructions proved wholly inaccurate, they stand in Sydenham to this day, mute witnesses to a pioneering attempt to popularize dinosaurs.

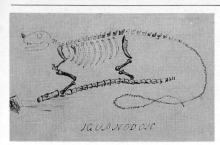

IGUANODON

Advancement of Science in Plymouth, he gave the Monarchs of the Mesozoic their official name. Combining the Greek roots

The interests of the brilliant anatomist and palaeontologist Richard Owen (1804–92) ranged well beyond dinosaurs. He could hold lengthy discussions on any fossil vertebrate, such as this enormous extinct bird, the moa, from New Zealand.

*deinos* ('terrible') and *sauros* ('lizard', in the general sense of 'reptile'), he grouped them under the heading 'Dinosauria' and published the word for the first time the following year. One hundred and fifty years later this scientific term, perhaps more than any other, continues to hold people spellbound.

## How the West was won – by scientists like Ferdinand V. Hayden

In the middle of the 19th century a sizable part of North America remained unexplored. From 1855 on the indefatigable palaeontologist Ferdinand V. Hayden scoured areas west of the Mississippi, and in what is now Montana he collected several fossilized teeth so odd looking that he felt they warranted further analysis. The following year, Joseph Leidy, an anatomist from Philadelphia, identified them as dinosaur teeth. Some were attributed to a herbivore akin to *Iguanodon*, others to a carnivore akin to *Megalosaurus*. Leidy named them *Trachodon* and *Deinodon*, respectively.

This scene from Late Cretaceous North America is one of Zdeněk Burian's best-known paintings. We can even pinpoint the time of the action, since the three genera depicted – left to right, *Trachodon* (*Anatosaurus*), *Tyrannosaurus* and *Struthiomimus* – could have coexisted only for a brief period seventy million years ago. 'The appearance of a *Tyrannosaurus* always struck terror into the other saurians. Some of these tried to save themselves in the swamps (for instance, the trachodontids), others fled in horror from the place of danger (as for instance the strange saurians of the genus *Struthiomimus*, resembling ostriches minus feathers), for the enormous power of these gigantic and heavy beasts of prey could not be resisted' (from *Prehistoric Animals*, Augusta and Burian, 1956). Today, however, the consensus among many specialists is that *Tyrannosaurus* was probably more of a scavenger than a predator.

## Joseph Leidy and *Hadrosaurus*: the first scientific description of a North American dinosaur

In 1858 William Parker Foulke, a distinguished fellow of the Academy of Natural Sciences in Philadelphia, spent some time in Haddonfield, New Jersey. A neighbour of his, John E. Hopkins, had found some curious fossilized vertebrae on his property about twenty years earlier and since then had been giving them away to friends as they passed through. Hopkins showed him where he had made his discovery and gave Foulke permission to start digging at the site.

The search turned up a number of large bones, and it fell to Leidy to tell the scientific community about the first partial skeleton of an American dinosaur, *Hadrosaurus*. He did more than just name the animal and describe bones; he also wrote about its posture and living habits. This time, the perceptive Leidy strayed from Richard Owen's model; he realized that *Hadrosaurus* was bipedal.

Although, after more than a century of debate, experts now reject his view that it led an amphibious life, Leidy must still be credited with being a pioneer in the field of dinosaur re-creation.

Born in 1831 in upstate New York, Othniel Charles Marsh (left) led many palaeontological expeditions to the West, where members of his crew (below, with Marsh in the centre) wielded a pick in one hand and a rifle in the other, theoretically to deter Indians but also to keep over-inquisitive rivals at bay.

**The rivalry between Othniel Charles Marsh and Edward Drinker Cope quickens the pace of discoveries in North America**

Two very different men with the same obsession – to be the first to find and describe new fossils – Marsh and Cope spent their lives and fortunes indulging their mutual passion.

They were on amicable terms at first but saw each other as potential rivals. The decisive incident took place in 1870, when Cope showed his colleague a plesiosaur skeleton he had described a few years earlier. Marsh examined it and pointed out that Cope had mistakenly placed the animal's head at the tip of its tail. Cope never recovered from this blow to his pride. Now the two adversaries proceeded to create a network of scouts and spies. Digging crews were equipped and kept ready to be the first at the scene as Cope and Marsh carried on dig

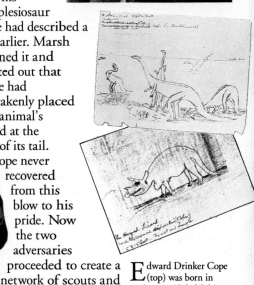

Edward Drinker Cope (top) was born in 1840 near Philadelphia. By the end of his life he had turned out an incredible fourteen hundred scientific articles – and sunk his entire fortune into dinosaur hunting. Above are two of his drawings.

Barnum Brown's flatboat proved efficient for scouting hundreds of kilometres of riverbank bluffs. Charles Sternberg and his sons followed suit in 1913; but there was no professional jealousy on the part of Brown, who rightly believed that the region held enough treasures for two crews. This led to the excavation of several hundred theropod, ceratopsian and hadrosaur skulls and skeletons.

after dig across the West. The so-called Bone Wars reached their climax in 1877 when two employees of the Union Pacific Railroad discovered a fabulous fossil bed at Como Bluff, a ridge in southern Wyoming. The richness of this bed made the palaeontologists' previous finds pale in comparison. Marsh's frenetic digging and collecting campaign at the site lasted for more than ten years.

Cope and Marsh's fanatical quest finally came to an end with their deaths in 1897 and 1899, respectively. Between the two of them, they had described more than 130 dinosaur species and amassed fabulous collections from several Western states.

Impressions of dinosaur skin (above right) are rare, and complete mummies (below) hardly ever turn up. Before it was entombed in sand, this *Anatosaurus* carcass underwent natural changes only an arid climate could have made possible.

Two great figures in palaeontology, Henry Fairfield Osborn and Barnum Brown, coax *Diplodocus* out of a Wyoming rockface, 1897 (right).

## Mummies and a floating search for dinosaurs

Marsh and Cope were gone, but the search continued uninterrupted. Distinguished fossil hunters carried on where they had left off. In the early 1900s Cope's former assistant, Charles Hazlius Sternberg, assisted by his three sons, conducted freelance expeditions in Alberta, Kansas,

Montana and Wyoming. Perhaps their best year was 1908, for while digging that summer in Wyoming, they discovered the first preserved impression of dinosaur skin – an actual fossilized 'mummy' of a duck-billed dinosaur. Two years later they found another specimen at about the same place.

Meanwhile, in 1910, Barnum Brown scouted the bluffs along the Red Deer River from Montana to Alberta, drifting downstream on a large flatboat that served as a combined camp and laboratory. The expedition proved such a success and yielded so many dinosaur remains that Brown went on to use the same technique several seasons in a row, swarms of troublesome mosquitoes notwithstanding!

## Palaeontological theories receive a jolt from a herd of ornithopods

The Old World garnered its share of discoveries, too, albeit at a less spirited

pace. In April 1878 the little Belgian mining town of Bernissart was thrust into the palaeontological limelight.

Coal miners working 322 metres down the Sainte-Barbe shaft hit a pocket of marl containing fossil bones. Workers had found fossilized bones or plants before, but never so many in so compact an area. It turned out that they had just tunnelled right through the skeleton of a large reptile. The management of the mine quickly notified what was then the Belgian Museum of Natural History. More than thirty *Iguanodon* skeletons and many other fossils were unearthed under the supervision of Louis de Pauw, the museum's engineer, then examined and described by Louis Dollo.

What danger sent this pair of *Iguanodons* scurrying for their lives? There was once speculation that the numerous skeletons at Bernissart, Belgium, were the remains of a herd that had rushed headlong into a ravine to escape predators. Today, however, the material is believed to have accumulated over a longer period.

If diggers working above ground sometimes have to brave gruelling conditions, imagine extracting tons of dinosaur bones from the bottom of a mine shaft! But, before anything was moved, extremely precise diagrams of the bones' original positions were made to ensure accurate reassembly in the laboratory. This drawing by G. Lavalette (1882) shows an *Iguanodon* as found in its fossil bed. This artist's fine work, like that of Louis de Pauw and Louis Dollo, helped to make the *Iguanodons* of Bernissart famous.

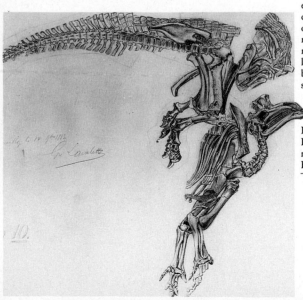

It took many years to restore and assemble the Bernissart dinosaurs, especially since the bones first had to be treated for 'pyrite disease' – a physicochemical process by which the iron pyrites in fossil bones cause them slowly to disintegrate when exposed to air. Several different 'cures' were attempted before the insidious disease eating away at the fossils could be brought under control. Today, visitors in Belgium's Royal Institute of Natural Sciences still must view the skeletons through huge display cases that are closely monitored for correct temperature and humidity. This picture shows the first specimen of *Iguanodon bernissartensis* being assembled in a makeshift workshop in Saint George's Chapel, Brussels. Palaeontologist Louis Dollo used this herd of dinosaurs as the basis for detailed descriptions of *Iguanodon*'s anatomy and biology, and specialists refer to his many scientific articles to this day.

## Fossil hunters head for Africa and Asia in the early 1900s

Extraordinary finds turned up on other continents too. Gigantic fossil bones were discovered in 1907 at Tendaguru, in what is now Tanzania. From 1908 to 1912 Edwin Hennig and Werner Janensch from the Museum of Natural History in Berlin worked these rich deposits and unearthed the remains of huge brachiosaurs and the small stegosaur *Kentrosaurus*.

Then palaeontologists set their sights on Asia. To this day the Gobi Desert is famous for the *Protoceratops* eggs and nests and the great many dinosaur skeletons Roy Chapman Andrews of the

American Museum of Natural History and his team found during their pioneering expeditions in Mongolia (1922–5). Soviet expeditions in 1946 and 1948, followed by Russo-Mongolian and Polish-Mongolian expeditions in the 1960s and 1970s, helped to turn the Gobi Desert into a heaven on earth for dinosaur hunters.

During the second half of the 20th century, China – land of dragons – took centre stage as the world learned of its rich and varied dinosaur fauna. The Russians conducted a number of early expeditions (1915–7), but in 1933 the Chinese continued the work on their own, spurred by C. C. Young (Yang Zhong-jian), the father of vertebrate palaeontology in China. The search for material has

A *Protoceratops andrewsi* skull from the Gobi Desert. The purpose of its bony neck frill – and that of all ceratopsians – still puzzles palaeontologists. Did it simply shield the neck, or did it provide a significantly enlarged attachment surface for jaw muscles?

When Roy Chapman Andrews (shown here holding two *Protoceratops* eggs) and a team of experts ventured into Mongolia under the auspices of the American Museum of Natural History, their chief objective was to find fresh evidence concerning human origins. For the most part, they found dinosaurs instead. The dinosaur species that laid these eggs was named *Protoceratops andrewsi* in honour of the expedition leader.

intensified since the creation of the People's Republic, and most of China's provinces now boast at least one *kong long*, or 'terrible dragon'.

## The age of pioneers is behind us, but not the age of discovery

The individuals mentioned in this chapter are just a few of the many people who, for more than a century and a half, have come under the spell of the terrible lizards of the Mesozoic. Today more than ever, the search goes on in different ways and with different means – but always with the goal of discovering and deciphering the record of the rocks. Whether in small groups or large-scale missions, people from all over the world – from Canada to Australia, from Patagonia to the USSR – are doing their utmost to bring dinosaurs back to life. The only thing they can count on is that there are many discoveries yet to come.

New and surprising specimens are still turning up in China, where practically all dinosaur families are represented. For Professor Dong Zhiming of Beijing, the hundreds of dinosaurs documented so far – for example, the sauropod *Mamenchisaurus*, the prosauropod *Lufengosaurus*, the stegosaur *Tuojiangosaurus* and the hadrosaur *Tsintaosaurus* – are just a few of the treasures in the rocks of his homeland.

### In the field

Though tools have changed since the turn of the century, much else about an excavation campaign remains the same. Weeks or even months of life in the field, subject to occasionally adverse conditions, required planning, however minimal, in order for diggers to get their work done. Crews still go through the same motions. This photograph shows the distribution centre for the tools and crates needed to unearth and transport dinosaur bones, as well as everything required for the crew's physical well-being on a turn-of-the-century expedition to Como Bluff. Here, Jacob Wortman and Walter Granger, the expedition leaders, partake of a frugal meal in their 'canvas dining room'.

## The dig

Dinosaur remains do not always lie flat. The buckling of the earth's crust in some places has caused geological strata to tilt to a nearly vertical position, as we see in this fossil-bearing rockface in what is now Dinosaur National Monument, Utah. Extracting a large dinosaur skeleton from the ground can take several weeks, assuming it is done with great care. Once removed, the bones, together with their rock matrix, are wrapped in plaster-dipped strips of burlap and allowed to harden into a stiff cast to prevent breakage during transport. Perfected by Arthur Lakes in 1877, this technique is used to this day, although hoisting apparatus has improved and horse-drawn wagons have given way to all-terrain vehicles.

As with everything the natural sciences scrutinize, dinosaurs have to be classified. To put it more precisely, people need a system of classification to help them to determine the connections among living creatures and to understand their degree of evolutionary interrelationship. But before dinosaurs can be incorporated into the tree of life, they must first be described.

CHAPTER 3

# THE NATURAL HISTORY OF AN AVERAGE DINOSAUR

*Dromiceiomimus* belonged to the intriguing theropod family known as ornithomimids. These ostrich-like dinosaurs were completely toothless, and their diet remains a mystery. They lived in Late Cretaceous times, and their remains have been found in Alberta.

## Description and classification: what is a dinosaur?

Dinosaurs belong to the class Reptilia and the subgroup of diapsid reptiles, which have a pair of openings in the skull behind each eye socket. During the Triassic, small diapsid reptiles called thecodonts gave rise to the pterosaurs (flying reptiles), crocodiles and two groups of dinosaurs, the saurischians and the ornithiscians. These four groups are collectively known as archosaurs (ruling reptiles), the ancestors of the birds. Crocodiles are the only reptilian representatives of the archosaurs alive today.

   In what respects did dinosaurs differ from the other archosaurs? For one thing, they were exclusively land-dwelling. More importantly, however, the limbs of dinosaurs were upright. Whereas reptilian limbs are normally splayed out to the side or semi-erect, dinosaur legs, like those of mammals and birds, were brought in beneath the body. This unique characteristic led to significant anatomical changes that made it possible to identify dinosaur bones.

## Dinosaurs are not a homogeneous group

In 1887 Harry Govier Seeley, dissatisfied with the classifications Marsh, Cope and Thomas Henry Huxley had proposed, realized that the term 'dinosaur' masked two different zoological orders. The main criterion for telling them apart is the structure of the pelvic girdle, which in reptiles

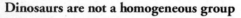

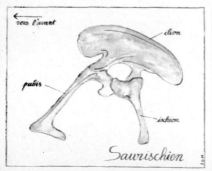

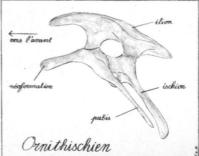

consists of the ilium, the pubis and the ischium. In some dinosaurs the three bones point in different directions – the normal reptilian build – and these Seeley called saurischians, or 'lizard-hipped'. In ornithischian ('bird-hipped') dinosaurs, both the pubis and ischium point downward and backward (although in many later types the pubis evolved a forward-pointing pronglike extension). The similarity to bird pelvises is, in fact, superficial; but the name stuck just the same.

Ornithischians share a number of other anatomical similarities, the most remarkable of which is the predentary, an extra bone at the front of the lower jaw.

In 1890 Albert Gaudry wrote,'Hermann von Meyer called them pachypods ("thick-footed") to indicate that, unlike living reptiles, they stood securely on massive, pillar-like feet. Richard Owen named them dinosaurs because several of them were gigantic in size. Thomas Henry Huxley classified them as Ornithoscelidae ("bird-thighed"), an allusion to their birdlike feature.' Nowadays experts hardly use the word 'dinosaur' anymore. They prefer the labels 'saurischian' (prosauropods, sauropods, theropods) and 'ornithischian' (ceratopsians, ornithopods, stegosaurs, ankylosaurs).

The *Ouranosaurus* skeleton in the natural history museum in Venice was found in 1966 in the Ténéré Desert, Niger. This large iguanodont (seven metres long) is so far the only ornithischian known to have had a dorsal 'sail'.

Saurischian and ornithischian hipbones (opposite).

After Andrew Carnegie gave France a plaster cast of *Diplodocus*, reassembling the skeleton was a national event. This photograph was taken a few days before French president Armand Fallières unveiled it on 15 June 1908. The three leading scientists seated in the foreground are (left to right) Arthur Coggeshall and William J. Holland of the Carnegie Museum and Marcellin Boule, a palaeontologist affiliated with the Museum of Natural History in Paris. Putting the skeleton on public display was the final step in a process that included a laborious description of individual pieces. For the sake of thoroughness, each and every bone was drawn and photographed.

### From bones to final reconstruction: painstaking work that requires a thorough command of anatomy

Palaeontologists start with nothing more than a skeleton or, as is more often the case, part of a skeleton. Therefore, the first stage in 'resurrecting' a dinosaur consists of reconstructing its framework of bones. After specialists have restored and identified the bones, they compare their findings with known data and fit them together, picking up useful clues along the way.

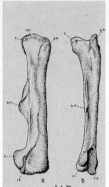

But bones reveal a great deal more. To varying degrees, they bear telltale marks showing where muscles and ligaments may have been attached. By comparing their location, size and direction with what they know about present-day reptiles, specialists can get a fairly accurate idea of the structure of major muscle groups. A static skeleton is thus fleshed out into a kind of anatomical figure which, to all intents and purposes, can move.

Of course, internal organs cannot be reconstructed in any detail. Decisions about body covering are based on fossil impressions of skin – the famous dinosaur 'mummies'. Pigmentation, however, is pure guesswork and must be inferred from the skin of living reptiles; restorers are somewhat hesitant about using bright colours.

## What do they eat?

Reconstructing an extinct animal also involves biology. The mere mention of dinosaurs' feeding habits conjures up the

Putting the right bone in the right place is not always as easy and obvious as it may seem, even for experts. Generally speaking, the initial phase of reconstructing a large dinosaur skeleton is rather like piecing together a gigantic jigsaw puzzle. Although mistakes in assembly are relatively uncommon, it can be difficult to tell whether or not certain bones (tail vertebrae, ribs, phalanges) have been correctly positioned.

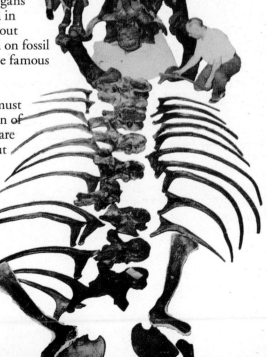

The smile of *Tyrannosaurus rex*, star dinosaur of the prehistoric bestiary, is enough to rivet anyone's attention – some of its daggerlike teeth are more than fifteen cm long. Whether they tore flesh or chewed plants, dinosaur teeth never cease to fascinate experts and laypeople alike. Three theropod teeth from the Sahara (below left) are every bit as intriguing as a much bigger *Megalosaurus* tooth from the Jura Mountains or a partial tooth row from a hadrosaur found in a Canadian deposit (bottom).

terrifying jaws of *Tyrannosaurus*. But it would be a mistake to think of all dinosaurs as fearsome flesh eaters. Actually, the few carnivorous varieties known to have existed were limited to the theropod group. Although some genera had a mixed diet, the majority of dinosaurs were herbivorous.

Close examination of dinosaurs' jaws provides our initial clues to their feeding habits. Unlike mammals, but like their fellow reptiles, dinosaurs had a homodont dentition, meaning that their teeth were uniform or nearly uniform regardless of their position in the tooth row.

Generally speaking, carnivorous dinosaurs had

powerfully built jaws lined with a single row of slicing, daggerlike teeth. In most instances, at least one of the two tooth ridges was finely serrated. This allowed for more effective slicing action through chunks of flesh, which, since carnivorous dinosaurs had no chewing teeth, had to be swallowed whole.

# Digesting the indigestible: herbivores evolve an extraordinary range of teeth

Feeding on plants presented vegetarians with a certain number of problems due to the presence of tough, abrasive, indigestible substances like cellulose or wood fibre.

The biggest dinosaurs, the sauropods, had only a few teeth in a single row, peg- or spoon-shaped (depending on family), and arranged in the front of the mouth like the teeth of a comb. This configuration enabled them to crop enough foliage or buds to sustain their multi-ton bodies.

Conversely, hadrosaurs (duck-billed dinosaurs) had no teeth in the front of the mouth; instead, there were impressive batteries of several hundred tightly packed, interlocking cheek teeth. This coarse grating surface, with new teeth continuously replacing old, could shred even the toughest plant material, such as pine needles. Ceratopsians had a sturdy beak for chopping off tough plants, and this was backed up by rows of powerful teeth that worked like the blades of shears. Ankylosaurs, however, had small, weak teeth unsuitable for anything but soft plants.

## Other clues shed light on the eating habits of dinosaurs

Dinosaurs unable to chew their food swallowed stones that ground it up in a specialized part of the stomach. (Modern birds hold stones in their gizzards for the same purpose.) Recently, a multidisciplinary team of scientists measured the abundance ratio of certain elements extracted from the fossilized collagen of a hadrosaur and showed that its diet consisted of dry-land plants, not aquatic vegetation, as had long been thought.

The surest way to prove what a dinosaur ate is to find out what was in its belly. In this respect the second specimen of *Compsognathus* ever to be found (1971, limestone, southeastern France) proved as remarkable as its 1859 Bavarian counterpart. Its fossilized stomach contents were first believed to be the skeleton of a fetus, but those tiny bones have now been identified as the remains of small reptiles akin to modern lizards.

## Eleanor Kish

The luminous paintings of Eleanor Kish have been instrumental in generating fresh interest in dinosaurs over the last ten years. Breaking with the traditional portrayal of certain dinosaurs, Kish has managed to combine artistic ability with the very latest scientific findings. As her longstanding associate, Canadian palaeontologist Dale A. Russell, once put it, 'She is the [palaeontologist's] eye upon a vanished world, and to her brush he owes images of landscapes he can never see.' Here the duck-billed dinosaur *Saurolophus* ventures into the water while a plesiosaur swims in the distance. Pages 56–7: another crested hadrosaur, *Hypacrosaurus*, browses at the edge of a dense forest. Pages 58–9: the fearsome *Daspletosaurus*, whose diminutive arms attest to a close kinship with *Tyrannosaurus*, glances menacingly at *Champsosaurus*, a crocodile-like rhynchocephalian.

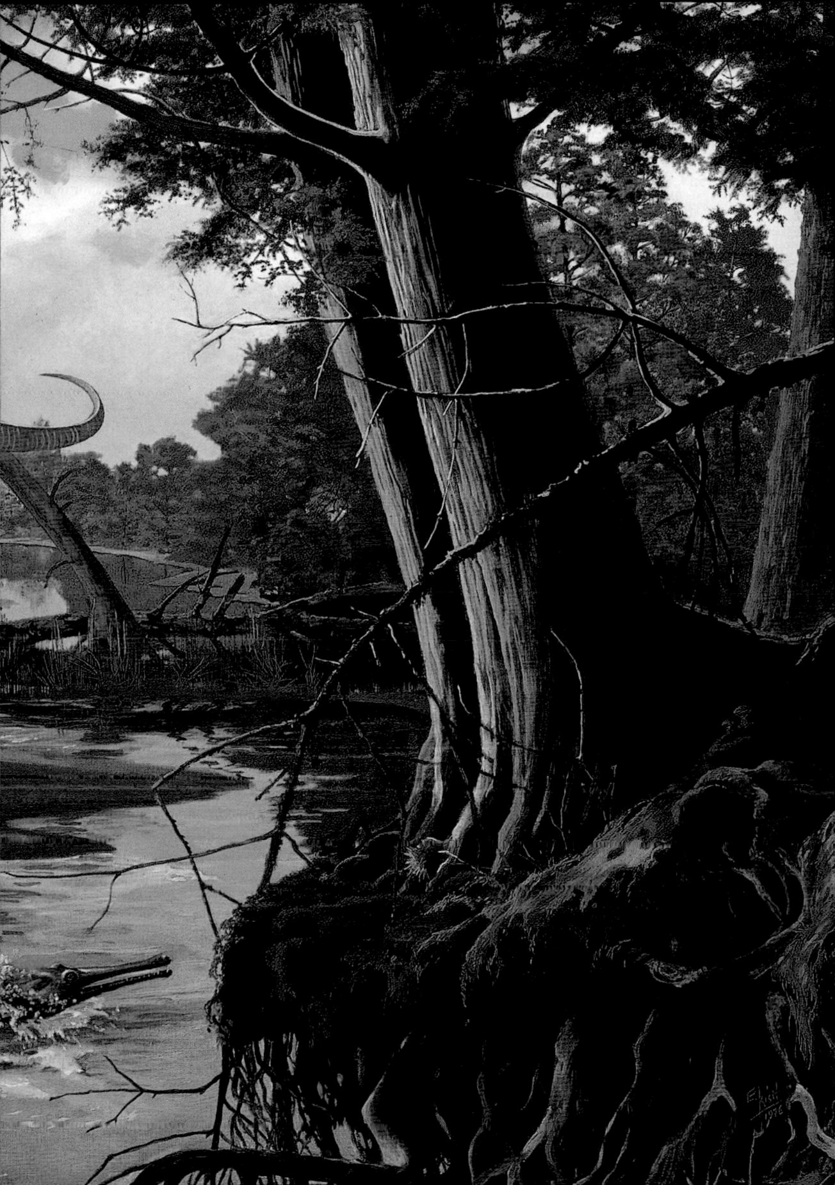

## When it comes to locomotion, dinosaurs run the gamut

Some, like carnivores that had to run down prey and keep forelimbs free for grasping, were two-legged; so were certain herbivores whose sole defensive strategy was running away. (For dinosaurs, bipedality seems to have offered the quickest way to get about – just the opposite of mammals.)

Others, such as animals that grazed on low-growing plants, walked on all fours, including the bulky sauropods that were for so long shown floundering through lakes and swamps. Scientists simply could not conceive of such massive body weight supporting itself without being buoyed up by water.

Today the consensus among palaeontologists is that the sauropods may have occasionally ventured into the water but spent most of their time on dry land. Biomechanical studies have shown that their limbs were quite capable of supporting their enormous weight out of the water. Some could even rear up on their hind legs, using the tail as a prop, and pluck off treetop foliage that other animals simply could not reach.

## We know for a fact that some dinosaurs laid eggs

How can we discuss biology and not even touch on reproduction? The very thought of dinosaurs laying eggs may strike one as comical. However, this in itself should come as no surprise. Dinosaurs were reptiles, and reptiles invented the hard-

Whether they were laid by dinosaurs (*Hypselosaurus*, top; *Protoceratops*, middle) or snakes (below), reptilian eggs proved more a revolution than an evolution by ushering in a whole new way of coming into the world.

Amphibians must return to their watery habitat to breed. Reptiles freed themselves of this necessity by placing the required liquid inside the egg (amniotic fluid) and encasing it in a protective porous shell. The shell itself is a marvel of efficiency, for as it decalcifies it provides the embryo with essential minerals and becomes easier for the hatchling to break through.

shelled egg. (Besides, there are even instances of ovoviviparity – eggs being hatched inside the mother's body, so the young are born live – among some present-day reptiles.) In the 1920s the Gobi Desert yielded a great many *Protoceratops* eggs and nests, as well as several skeletons belonging to this small ceratopsian. The female went to the trouble of digging a pit, which she then filled with eighteen to thirty eggs precisely arranged in concentric circles.

Like present-day crocodiles and birds, some dinosaurs cared for their young. We know this from an important nesting ground that was discovered in Montana in 1978 by palaeontologists John Horner and Robert Makela. One of the nests had a carefully built-up rim and was found to contain the

Some scientists have felt that brachiosaurs were able to live in much deeper waters than the brontosaurs and diplodoci. But to picture these giants completely submerged raises the question of how their chest and lungs withstood the water pressure.

Some experts with a stronger penchant for mathematics than palaeontology have calculated that particularly swift bipedal dinosaurs could reach top speeds of up to 50 kph. This estimate is plausible in the case of champion runners like the ornithomimids (ostrich dinosaurs), the family that included this pair of *Struthiomimus*. Their proportions were very similar to those of present-day ostriches, which can sprint at more than 40 kph.

fossil remains of some fifteen hadrosaur hatchlings. Nearby lay the skeleton of one of their parents, which was named, appropriately enough, *Maiasaura* ('good mother lizard'). Regardless of what may have happened to the parents, the hatchlings must have been nestbound by instinct.

### Sooner or later they must face the outside world – and run!

Carnivores ran to hunt; herbivores with no other means of defence ran to escape carnivores. Eat or be eaten. The most advanced adaptation to running is found among relatively lightweight bipedal animals no more than two or three metres long. Whether small, lightweight theropods, flesh-eating coelurosaurs, or agile ornithopods like the herbivorous hypsilophodonts, their hindlimb morphology is very similar. Sturdy hipbones; long, powerfully built legs; tapered feet; a gait in which the weight is placed mostly on the front of the foot (as found in the swiftest living mammals); bundles of tendons in the tail, allowing it to stiffen and counterbalance the front part of the body – combined, these characteristics enabled them to take long, quick, fluid strides.

## Four-legged herbivores are amazingly resourceful in avoiding being eaten

Every group perfected its own particular techniques. The sheer bulk of *Apatosaurus* (thirty metric tons) or even the somewhat less imposing *Diplodocus* (ten tons) may well have been enough to give a solitary theropod pause. The sight of *Diplodocus'* long whiplash tail cutting through the air would have kept all other would-be attackers at bay. The tails of some ornithischians fairly bristled with weaponry that could be swung from side to side by powerful muscles. Stegosaurs, for example, had tails armed with at least one, usually two, pairs of long, bony spikes covered with horn. Any aggressor's belly would have been an easy target!

The weaponry of medieval knights seems puny indeed compared with the tails of certain dinosaurs. Yet the bony remains of this daunting arsenal, be it the clubbed tail of ankylosaurs (above) or the long spikes of stegosaurs (left), represent only part of their defence system. We must also try to visualize the tremendous tail muscles that swung these weapons from side to side.

This was also the case with ankylosaurs. The long tails of *Euoplocephalus* and its armoured brethren were tipped with a club-like ball formed from two or three clumps of fused bone that could break the leg of any theropod. Moreover, ankylosaurs were encased in an impenetrable armour of sometimes very large, flat plates embedded in the skin. Some of these bony nodules extruded spikes that ran down the back, flanks and tail. When one of these living assault tanks flattened itself against the ground, even the strongest of carnivores would not have been able to get at its only vulnerable spot, the belly.

### The horns of some ceratopsians rival those of the best-endowed living bulls

Of course, the defensive arsenal of dinosaurs included horns. Ceratopsians had a characteristic bony frill that shielded the neck area. Although the defensive role of this sometimes sizable structure has been challenged by several experts, no such doubt

Unlike ankylosaurs (above), ceratopsians did not have a body armour of bony plates. This family is now divided into two groups: those with short frills that just covered the neck (for example, *Triceratops*, below) and those with long frills extending as far as the middle of the back. All ceratopsians wielded horns that varied in size depending on genus.

surrounds the one or more horns that jutted out from the heads of these dinosaurs. One of the best-known is the five and a half ton *Triceratops*, a very bulky Late Cretaceous ceratopsian. Its two long brow horns and shorter, thicker nose horn must have inflicted crippling or even mortal wounds on many a tyrannosaur.

*Iguanodon* had a characteristic that so far has not been found on any other dinosaur. Each of its 'thumbs' evolved into a prominent spike that stuck out as much as twenty cm – easily a match for theropod claws in hand-to-hand combat. Although carnivores were not the only dinosaurs with claws, theirs were designed specifically for aggression, that is to seize, hold and dismember prey. Thin, sharp and strongly curved, they resemble the talons of a bird of prey, especially since they are known to have had horny outer sheaths. In some cases a claw could be used as a lethal weapon in its own right.

One theropod of the dromaeosaur family, *Deinonychus* ('terrible claw'), probably used the very large, sickle-shaped claw on the second toe of each foot to slash through its victims' bellies. The claws of some herbivorous dinosaurs, on the other hand, were broader, blunter and not as strongly curved. Although we cannot rule out their use as defensive weapons, they must have been used chiefly for foraging and grasping food.

### An extraordinary find in the Gobi Desert: two dinosaurs locked in death after a no-win fight to the finish

In 1971 members of a Polish-Mongolian expedition unearthed two fossils that told of a drama played out in Late Cretaceous times. A small dromaeosaur *Velociraptor* had died with its claws embedded in the head shield of *Protoceratops*. Did the two animals succumb to exhaustion or

A lthough the bony claws of dinosaurs come in a variety of shapes and sizes, reflecting different life-styles and diets, they all have the same basic structure. Their length, degree of curvature, thickness and mobility are group-specific: witness these two theropod claws from the

Sahara (top). Below them is the third phalanx of a hadrosaur toe that is altogether different in form and function. Here, locomotion completely superseded offensive or defensive use.

wounds after a long, drawn-out struggle? Did some outside cause bring about their simultaneous deaths? We shall probably never find out.

More often than not, dinosaur bones bear telltale signs of less deadly encounters. For example, a bony callus can mark a fracture that mended while the animal was alive. Accidents? Battle scars? We can only speculate.

By the same token, how can we know whether bite marks were made by a predator or by a scavenger long after an animal's death? Less frequently, experts come across evidence of bone pathology. It is not unusual to find two or more ankylosed vertebrae in sauropod tails. Cancerous bone tumours, albeit rarer, have been identified in a few individuals. Tens of millions of years after a dinosaur's death, it is more common for its fossilized bones to tell us about its state of health than about the causes of its death.

D inosaur footprints generally create headaches for specialists. Not so for little Tommy Pendley, the son of a palaeontologist working at the Paluxy River site (now in Dinosaur Valley State Park near Glen Rose, Texas) in 1939. A single impression was just the right size for a cooling dip. This deposit is famous for the beautifully preserved tracks (right) created when a theropod (three-toed prints) tried to run down a sauropod (oval prints).

T he only fossil like it in the world, the entwined skeletons of *Protoceratops* and *Velociraptor* (left) tell us how dromaeosaurs (such as *Velociraptor*) killed their prey. They securely clutched the victim's head with their arms while ripping into its belly with the huge 'switchblade' claw on their second toe.

## Dinosaur footprints provide important clues to social behaviour

The peculiar fossils commonly known as dinosaur footprints have given rise to a special branch of palaeontology: palaeoichnology (the study of ancient tracks). Since bones were often moved by waterflow or scavengers, sometimes very far from where an animal died, a dinosaur's footprints are the only proof that it actually lived at a particular site. Although studying dinosaur tracks can be a tricky affair, in many cases it is still possible to determine, if nothing else, the group to which an individual belonged. Bipedal or quadrupedal gait, the presence of claws and the number, angle and size of fingers are a few of the

Mark Hallett's painting *The River* shows what a Late Jurassic pterosaur might have surveyed as it soared above what is now Utah, assuming that flying reptiles had colour vision. Lush vegetation thrived in what was then a hot, humid climate, and a large waterway would have attracted herbivores, with carnivores following close behind.

parameters used in identification. However, meaningful estimates of an animal's size, weight and speed cannot be made unless the tracks it left are extremely well preserved.

Late Jurassic deposits along the Purgatory River in Colorado turned up more than thirteen hundred such footprints. Close analysis revealed that 140 million years ago a herd of sauropods lumbered along the steeply sloping shores of a lake, perhaps while migrating. They moved not as a disorganized horde, but as a tightly structured unit. The young (and pregnant females?) kept to the centre, surrounded by adults, with the strongest individuals stationed on the periphery. This communal defence strategy is still used by a number of large mammals today.

We can spot several different types of dinosaurs. Most of the *Diplodocus* herd (left) has safely crossed the river; a pair of brachiosaurs (far left) watch as a straggler is cornered by three *Ceratosaurus* (centre). Small carnivorous *Ornitholestes* inspect some camasaur and stegosaur carcasses (right) while a solitary theropod (*Allosaurus*) looks on (far right).

It would be the height of pretence to claim we know all there is to know about dinosaurs. Not a month goes by when a dinosaur is not unearthed somewhere in the world, and with every discovery we have to revise much of our thinking. Palaeontologists do not usually unearth entire skeletons; they have to be satisfied with partial skeletons or even a few bones. Then the strange process of reconstructing the victim gets under way.

CHAPTER 4

# A CHALLENGE TO SCIENCE

Fossils displayed in halls of palaeontology, like this *Triceratops* skull, represent only a fraction of the collections available to scientists worldwide. Thousands of specimens are used primarily for research purposes. Painting of *Diplodocus* (left).

The fact that fossilization subjects bones to powerful mechanical stresses, often leaving them broken, crushed or misshapen, compounds an already difficult task. Specialists must allow for this in their research. If the skeletons of certain genera – *Allosaurus, Iguanodon* and *Triceratops*, among others – are familiar today, it is because they have been found in large quantities. The gaps in our knowledge of dinosaurs can only be filled through the repeated testing of successive models.

**Instead of scoffing at our predecessors' blunders, we should insist on their right to fallibility**

Not counting *Iguanodon*'s 'horn' (which turned out to be its thumb, misplaced), the most famous instance of this kind of mistake involved the brontosaur (correct scientific name: *Apatosaurus*). In 1879 Marsh reconstructed the partial skeleton of his brontosaur using a camasaur skull from a nearby fossil bed. This was not rectified until 1975. The correct head turned out to be similar to that of *Diplodocus* and therefore quite different from the skull that had been mistakenly attached to *Apatosaurus* for nearly a hundred years.

In the early 1900s palaeontologists often set up new dinosaur species on the evidence of scanty material, sometimes as little as a single vertebra or tooth. Therefore, remains of animals of what we now know to be the same species were often given different names. Now, before an animal can be assigned a new genus or species name, its remains must be compared with documented findings; in this way, individuals of the same species should always be given the same species name.

The celebrated *Megalosaurus* exemplifies this kind of confusion. Today there are eighteen species of

Two bone tumours, probably brought on by arthritis, occur a few vertebrae apart on the tail of a *Diplodocus* skeleton. A third such ankylosis around the first tail vertebrae of the same specimen suggests that in life this sauropod was crippled by disease.

*Megalosaurus* ranging from the Early Jurassic to the Late Cretaceous. Yet it is highly unlikely that a single genus could have endured for more than 100 million years. Lacking a precise description, *Megalosaurus* has become a catch-all term for the remains of large, unidentifiable theropods. Conversely, the abundance of *Triceratops* skulls and skeletons swelled this genus to fifteen species, eleven from the same geological formation in Wyoming and Montana. Today specialists find it inconceivable that so many different species could have evolved over so limited a period and area.

## The perennial problem of palaeontological species

The example of *Triceratops* brings us to one of the most critical problems facing dinosaur researchers today. Do minor differences in the bones of what appear to be two very similar dinosaurs constitute individual variations? Do they indicate different growth stages? Two different species within the same genus? Since there is no law that allows us to quantify intraspecific individual variations, definition of species – the smallest unit of classification – will continue to be the grist of contentious conferences for a long time to come.

*Megalosaurus* was a powerfully built bipedal flesh eater – one of the so-called carnosaurs – that measured five to nine metres in length, depending on species. At the present time several palaeontologists are attempting to restore a semblance of order to this indescribably muddled genus; but the fragmentary condition of most finds has made the job difficult, if not impossible. Some have been suggesting for a long time that the name *Megalosaurus* should be limited to dinosaurs from the Late Jurassic, and at least this is a step toward clarification. The inescapable fact is that, given what we currently know, palaeontologists are simply unable to assign genus names, much less species names, to animals that have left only scant remains. To avoid further confusion, it would be wise in such cases not to take classification beyond the family level.

Could such minor differences be indicative of sexual dimorphism within a single species? No, there is no way to draw conclusions about the sexual dimorphism of reptiles based solely on their skeletons. However, some have argued that hadrosaur crests are just such a marker, that lambeosaurine (crested) and hadrosaurine (flat-headed) duckbills were the males and females, respectively, of the hadrosaur family.

This hypothesis is no longer accepted because the former and latter do not necessarily turn up together in the various geological formations. Nevertheless, we have good reason to believe that, within the lambeosaur group, males had larger crests than females.

*Edaphosaurus* (above and *Dimetrodon* (not shown) are two of the best-known early mammal-like reptiles. Although both of these pelycosaurs were equipped with dorsal sails, they differed considerably in terms of anatomy and diet. The former fed on plants, while the latter was a ferocious carnivore.

## Beyond species: thermoregulation, an example of convergent evolution

While some dinosaurs sported odd-looking head ornaments, others boasted equally curious appendages on their backs, such as very long neural spines growing up and out from the vertebrae. Far from being eculiar to a single group or family, this specialization s an example of what palaeontologists refer to as onvergent evolution. Found in mammal-like reptiles ating back to Late Permian times (such as *Dimetrodon* and *Edaphosaurus*), this 'sail' has so far been found only in two very different dinosaurs: *Spinosaurus*, a theropod, and *Ouranosaurus*, an ornithopod.

Of all the hypotheses that have attempted to explain the purpose of this dorsal fin, body temperature regulation seems, for now, the most cogent. The capillaries coursing through the skin stretched over these vertebral extrusions may have been heat exchangers. Whenever an animal positioned itself at a right angle to the sun's rays, the sail would have worked like a solar heater, quickly warming blood that would then distribute absorbed heat throughout the body. At the hottest time of day it would lessen sail exposure by angling it away from the sun, or turn it into the slightest breeze, thereby dissipating heat for a cooling effect. The plates running down the backs of stegosaurs have a honeycomb structure that seems ill-suited to the defensive role long attributed to them. They may have worked in much the same way to regulate body temperature.

There is speculation that some dinosaurs had mechanisms to regulate body temperature. Examples include the dorsal plates of *Stegosaurus* (opposite below) and the 'sail' stretched over the long vertebral spines of the ornithopod *Ouranosaurus* (below) or the theropod *Spinosaurus*. This hypothesis figures prominently in the controversy pitting proponents of warm-blooded dinosaurs against those who hold the more orthodox view that they were cold-blooded, like modern reptiles. As with everything pertaining to the physiology of extinct organisms, definitive proof remains elusive. The plates running down the backs of some stegosaurs are very small or nothing more than long, spiky extrusions; it is difficult to conceive of them as heat exchangers, as some purport. But we must remember that nature never lets existing stuctures go to waste and adapts them to a purpose.

## Warm-blooded or cold-blooded? Experts are divided over dinosaur physiology

The concept of thermoregulatory adaptation is one of the most hotly debated issues surrounding dinosaur physiology. Modern reptiles commonly referred to as 'cold-blooded' of course do not actually have cold blood; their internal temperature fluctuates with that of their surroundings. For many years, Robert Bakker of the University of Colorado has been gathering evidence and advancing arguments to prove that dinosaurs were warm-blooded, that they generated and maintained a constant body temperature (endothermy, or homeothermy), the way birds and mammals do. His wide range of supporting data includes analysis of predator-prey ratios in animal populations, correlation between the estimated metabolism of certain theropods and their presumed levels of activity, and studies of bone tissue.

Enticing though these arguments may be, not all palaeontologists concur. Producing and maintaining a certain body temperature requires considerable expenditure of energy and presupposes a ready supply of oxygen and food that, through complex biochemical processes, can be transformed into heat.

The sauropod *Mamenchisaurus*, a member of the diplodocid family, was discovered in 1957 in Sichuan province, China, and took more than three months to excavate. Its completely restored skeleton is now on display in Beijing. Although remarkably long necks were a hallmark of all diplodocids, none could equal this one's for sheer disproportion.

It may be tempting to speculate that small carnivorous dinosaurs were warm-blooded, but it is harder to imagine how that would be the case with a thirty-ton sauropod – it seems inconsistent with the energy intake necessary and the feeding techniques available to this bulky creature. However, we must bear in mind that the bigger the animal, the more it is a *de facto* homeotherm, since its bulk-to-body-surface ratio causes it to lose or absorb heat far more slowly than a small animal would. Once again, the issue is complicated by the astonishing variety of dinosaurs.

## Some experts are getting at the heart of the matter – literally

Present-day warm-blooded animals – mammals and birds – have a heart with four fully partitioned

The neck alone, with its nineteen elongated cervical vertebrae, took up fully ten metres of this enormous creature's total length (tip of the snout to tip of the whiplash tail). The powerful neck muscles needed to move this living cantilever about are clearly visible in Mark Hallett's *Crossing the Flat* (1986), a painting in the Los Angeles County Museum of Natural History.

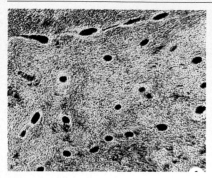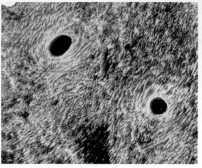

chambers, which prevents oxygen-rich blood flowing towards the organs from mixing with oxygen-depleted blood returning to the lungs. This seems to be a prerequisite for homeothermy, which uses up a great deal of oxygen. Even if one does not go along with Bakker's ideas – many palaeontologists don't – it is still plausible that dinosaurs had chambered hearts. A bulky sauropod would have to have had high blood pressure to pump blood to its brain, which could be more than ten metres higher than its heart. If its cardiac chambers were not fully partitioned, the resulting pressure in the lung area would have been dangerously high, even causing pulmonary capillaries to burst. Although no one has ever seen a dinosaur heart, many experts feel this is a sound hypothesis. Furthermore, such a heart would not be unique among reptiles, since crocodiles have (almost) fully partitioned hearts.

## We lack conclusive evidence about dinosaurs' growth rate and lifespan

This is an important question, particularly with regard to bulky dinosaurs. How did a newborn weighing a few kilos manage to acquire the size and weight of its multi-ton parents? It would have had to increase its

In most cases, the process of fossilization left intact the internal microstructure of bones and teeth. These two photos of thin sections of dentin from an *Ouranosaurus* tooth were taken using light microscopy, one in normal light (left), the other at a higher magnification in polarized light (right). Today, electron microscopes are commonly used to unlock the innermost secrets of dinosaur biology, although results have been known to fall short of expectations (in determining sauropod growth rates, for example). Palaeontological research is no longer limited to the surface aspects of dinosaur remains.

weight by a factor of as much as two or three thousand. If we use modern reptiles as our reference point, there are only two solutions. Either they grew slowly but over a very long period of time – perhaps more than a hundred years or so, the way some land-dwelling tortoises do – or they grew rapidly during the first few years of life. (As for the average lifespan of an individual, the notion that telltale growth rings may have been laid down at regular intervals in bone or dental tissue has always left some experts unconvinced.)

## Social behaviour and the importance of visual clues

Analysis of footprints has shown that some dinosaurs, capable of social behaviour, lived in organized herds. As in every population, there arises the question of how certain individuals achieved dominance within their group. Some palaeontologists now maintain that the neck frills of ceratopsians and various bony crests of lambeosaurs served as visual devices to signal recognition or dominance. The bigger (and perhaps even more colourful?) these appendages, the more dominant the animal. It is often thought that pachycephalosaurs used their thick, domed skulls as

Since pachycephalosaur remains are relatively scarce, we know little about this puzzling group of dinosaurs. Their distinguishing feature is a thickened skull cap, which in some genera formed an extraordinarily high dome of solid bone (witness this 23-cm-thick *Pachycephalosaurus* skull). These bipedal ornithischians, all from the Late Cretaceous except for one Early Cretaceous genus, are believed to have engaged in behaviour like that of present-day bighorn sheep.

*Apatosaurus*, previously known as *Brontosaurus* (below and left).

head-butting devices to establish pecking order, much as mountain goats do today. The thought of two ceratopsians locking horns during a ritualistic sparring match for territory or breeding partners is a far cry from the conventional image of sluggish, dim-witted dinosaurs.

## The widespread misconception about dinosaur 'stupidity'

The bulky sauropods had a few grams of grey matter – and enormous bodies. The record holder in this area is believed to be *Stegosaurus*, whose walnut-sized brain controlled more than two tons of flesh and blood. Yet this genus held on for more than ten million years during the Late Jurassic, proof that its brain was well adapted to its life-style. (Granted, herbivores such as *Stegosaurus* generally had less fully developed brains than flesh eaters. Hunting requires keen senses, cunning and quick reflexes. The brains of some small carnivorous dinosaurs were proportionately as large as those of modern birds.)

No one has ever found a fossilized dinosaur brain, and the chances are that no one ever will. For quite some time, however, we have had a fairly clear idea of what the grey matter of some dinosaurs looked like. As long as a braincase has not changed shape during fossilization, the cavity it surrounds can serve as a highly accurate mould of the brain. Left: this cast of a *Triceratops* brain shows enough detail to map out the areas of the animal's brain, deduce the origins of its twelve cranial nerves and make comparisons with modern reptiles.

The idea that dinosaurs had two brains, the second one purportedly located in their hindquarters, is yet another misconception, at best a distortion. The huge swelling of nervous tissue many dinosaurs had in the vicinity of the sacral vertebrae was, in fact, nothing more than a relay centre for the hip area, and elevating it to the status of a thinking brain would be an exaggeration.

In any event, how could the word 'stupid' apply to creatures that ruled the earth for nearly 150 million years?

### The mysterious sound of the Mesozoic: music to scientists' ears

On the surface, the very idea of re-creating a dinosaur call seems impracticable, if not preposterous. Yet there have been rigorously scientific attempts to do just that.

The elongated bony crest of some lambeosaurine duckbills was actually a hollow structure housing an air tube that connected the nasal cavity to the back of the throat. A number of hypotheses have been proposed concerning their function. David Weishampel of Philadelphia worked out a detailed reconstruction of how air would have moved through

The nose horn of *Monoclonius* (below right) or *Styracosaurus* (below left) must have been a fearsome weapon, but the spikes jutting from the edge of the latter's neck frill were used more for display than aggression. In other ceratopsian genera (for example, *Triceratops*), triangular knobs all around the edge of the neck frill gave it a scalloped look. Many palaeontologists now believe that frill size and ornamentation played a key role in ceratopsian social behaviour. The skin sheathing the neck frill may well have been brightly coloured, and that is how some illustrators visualize and depict it.

a lambeosaur's crest and analyzed its acoustical properties. He calculates that sound waves were emitted at frequencies ranging from 48 to 240 Hz – the sound may have resembled a medieval horn. Lambeosaurs' hadrosaurine cousins weren't necessarily relegated to silence, either. There is speculation that their flat snouts were covered with an inflatable flap or pouch of skin – perhaps, as in modern nature, it was brightly coloured – which may have been used to signal anger or sexual desire both visually and acoustically. Even the vocalizations of dinosaurs have come under scientific scrutiny. After all, why should we assume that the world of the dinosaurs was as hushed as our halls of palaeontology?

The long, tubelike structure protruding from the head of *Parasaurolophus*, a Late Cretaceous lambeosaur (crested hadrosaur), has been variously identified as a snorkel, a branch deflector, a tremendous extension of the nasal mucosa and, more recently, a device for amplifying vocalizations. The 'call' *Parasaurolophus* let out under certain conditions may have sounded like the music produced by the trio of krummhorn players below.

## Perhaps dinosaurs did not completely die out at the end of the Mesozoic

If someone were to mention during Christmas dinner that the expertly roasted turkey was actually a feathered dinosaur, it would be dismissed as a facetious remark worthy of a slightly tipsy palaeontologist. Yet one of the three decidedly unfacetious hypotheses concerning the origin of birds could almost be put that way. The fact that scales cover the legs of birds and that the modified scales we call feathers cover the rest of their

The industrialist Werner Siemens bought this remarkable specimen of *Archaeopteryx* for 20,000 marks shortly after its discovery in 1877 near Eichstätt, about twenty km east of Solnhofen, a rich source of fossils; it is now in Berlin's Humboldt University Museum. The chronicle of what is still considered the oldest known bird began with a solitary feather found in 1860. The first skeleton was discovered a year later and bought by the British Museum in London. Five more specimens have since been unearthed, the most recent in late 1987. All of them come from the same 140-million-year-old Late Jurassic layer as the Bavarian specimen of *Compsognathus*, which is structurally quite similar to the proto-bird. In fact, the *Archaeopteryx* specimen in the museum at Eichstätt, discovered in 1950 and thought at the time to be a juvenile form of this small theropod, was not correctly identified until 1973.

bodies argues in favour of their reptilian ancestry. But is the ancestor of modern birds to be found among the thecodonts (early crocodile-like reptiles) or the dinosaurs? That is the question dividing specialists. As for the dinosaurian ancestry of birds, no one is saying that *Diplodocus* or *Triceratops* could have conceivably transformed itself into a sparrow. At the heart of the controversy lies *Archaeopteryx*, the oldest known bird. This Late Jurassic creature has quite a few anatomical features in common with the small, agile running theropods traditionally grouped under the heading coelurosaurs.

Like many issues surrounding dinosaurs, this one is far from being settled because the fossil record is so incomplete. Just the same, many palaeontologists believe that dinosaurs are still among us, thanks to a specialized evolutionary line radiating from the small coelurosaurs of Triassic or Early Jurassic times.

Why did the dinosaurs die out? Their mysterious extinction reinforces our simplified view of them as unadaptable creatures. But the earth the dinosaurs roamed was in constant flux. Enduring for 150 million years was no mean feat: in this time continents drifted, and, about 120 million years ago, plant life, the primary food source of most dinosaurs, underwent a sweeping transformation.

CHAPTER 5

## DINOSAUR LIFE IN AN EVER-CHANGING WORLD

When fossilized plants, like this fern frond, are preserved well enough to be identified (*Flabellaria*), they have a great deal to tell us. Left: *Edmontosaurus*.

### The probable connection between the gradual revolution in plant life and the emergence of new dinosaur families

The horsetails, cycads, treelike ferns and conifers that made up the bulk of continental plant life until Late Jurassic times gradually gave way to the angiosperms – flowering plants – a category of flora destined to enjoy ever-increasing success. They are known to have emerged about the middle of the Early Cretaceous; their pollen has been found in deposits from this period. However, the plants themselves do not make their first indisputable appearance in the fossil record until the Late Cretaceous.

Some of these pioneering families – magnolias, dogwoods, oaks, willows and birches – are still represented in modern nature. During the second half of the Cretaceous, ceratopsians, ankylosaurs, pachycephalosaurs and hadrosaurs filled ecological niches left empty by other herbivorous dinosaurs such as brachiosaurs and stegosaurs.

Horsetails (left, above) are still found today, but they are far less conspicuous and varied than they were during the age of dinosaurs. Petrified fronds attest to the antiquity of ferns, which seem to have fared better against the invading angiosperms. A persistent line dating back to Palaeozoic times – well before the dinosaurs – ferns evolved an extraordinarily wide range of forms. Witness these two fossilized fronds from the Mesozoic, one (left, below) from the Jurassic-Cretaceous transition in France, the other from the Jurassic in southeast Asia (below).

### Dinosaur populations and migrations as palaeogeographic clues

Geologists and palaeontologists have long noted a degree of similarity between dinosaur faunas on different continents. As early as

1912, German meteorologist Alfred Wegener used this phenomenon as a supporting argument for his theory of continental drift. The parallels between the dinosaur populations of Madagascar, India and Patagonia did not come about by chance.

Now universally accepted but better known as 'plate tectonics' (a reference to its governing mechanism), continental drift produced a major geological realignment during the reign of the dinosaurs. In Triassic times all exposed landmasses were united into the supercontinent of Pangaea. The gradual opening up of the oceans caused this immense monolith to break up throughout the Mesozoic era.

Some 64 million years ago the surface of the Earth already looked more or less as it does today. In recent years comparative studies of dinosaur fossils from Early Cretaceous Africa (particularly Niger and Cameroon) and counterparts from Brazil have been presented as crucial palaeontological evidence in determining exactly when the South Atlantic opened up. Likewise, the distribution of various Late Cretaceous dinosaur groups indicates that certain continents, now unattached, were once connected by land bridges.

Thus, dinosaur migrations are being used to test palaeogeographic models. Conversely, the early geographic isolation of certain areas of the globe

Occasionally, fossilization preserves so many details that it is possible to identify the genus and species of certain plants accurately. Note the fossilized stamens in these blossoms of *Bombax sepultiflorum* (left), an angiosperm from the Oligocene (Tertiary period). The emergence and explosive spread of flowering plants during the Cretaceous must have had considerable impact on the feeding habits of plant-eating dinosaurs. Now prized for their large, showy blossoms, the magnolias (below),

one of the earliest angiosperm families to conquer the globe, may have been part of the diet of some Mesozoic herbivores.

allowed dinosaur populations to diversify and evolve along different paths from those on major continental landmasses.

## The extinction of the dinosaurs: the facts of the matter

If the 150-million-year rule of the dinosaurs has assumed virtually mythic proportions in the minds of fascinated humans, the great reptiles' extinction has simply enhanced their reputation. For the general public, it is undoubtedly one of the most intriguing of all scientific riddles. Yet the same mystery surrounds the dying out of many other zoological groups throughout the history of life.

Laypeople are far less interested in the mass extinctions that marked the transition between the Permian and the Triassic about 250 million years ago. The disappearance of the Monarchs of the Mesozoic often overshadows the many other groups that died out when they did. Pterosaurs, ichthyosaurs, mosasaurs, plesiosaurs, numerous

A pachycephalosaur ('thick-headed lizard') peeps out at us from beneath lush vegetation after taking cover during a Late Cretaceous downpour. In another age, this painting by Eleanor Kish might have been interpreted as a scene from the flood of Genesis. Torrential rains spelled the end of the world – such is the vision that haunted ancient commentators, whose outlook was generally more mystical than scientific.

marine invertebrates (ammonites, belemnites and rudistids) – none of them survived the transition between the Cretaceous and the Tertiary 64.5 million years ago. However, the notion of a sudden, simultaneous, worldwide extinction remains unconfirmed. Were all dinosaurs wiped out at the same time by some sweeping catastrophic event, or did they fall prey to a slow, inexorable decline? Neither theory can be conclusively proven. Although (at the last count) more than sixty theories purporting to explain this phenomenon have been advanced, not a single one fully satisfies all palaeontologists.

Nowadays, biblical floods no longer satisfy our need to know what killed off the dinosaurs. If the issue of the dinosaurs' demise has been deluged by anything, it is by the pseudo-scientific hypotheses that claim to explain it.

**More than sixty theories, from the far-fetched to the scientifically sound**

Whether catastrophistic or gradualistic, these hypotheses, needless to say, vary tremendously in scientific value. Many of them confirm nothing more than the unbridled imagination of their proponents. This constellation of theories, ranging from the deadly serious to the wildly preposterous, can be broken into seven main categories.

Hypotheses alleging food-related causes include lack or oversupply of food, destruction of certain plants by insects and poisoning due to the presence of toxic substances in plants. Some speculate that we need look no farther than the dinosaurs themselves: 'racial' senility, malfunctioning metabolism, heart disease, the failure of eggs to hatch and even suicidal tendencies brought on by overwhelming melancholy or stupidity. For others, the key to the mystery is biological onslaught: epidemics, parasites, elimination of all herbivorous dinosaurs by carnivores that then preyed on each other, diminutive mammals driven by starvation to gorge themselves on the eggs of large reptiles. Warming, cooling, floods and droughts sum up climate-related arguments. Geological and atmospheric explanations are, if nothing else, more numerous: volcanic dust, poisonous gases, shifts in the Earth's rotational axis, mountain uplift, extraction of the moon from the Pacific Basin, retreats or encroachments of the sea. Astronomical causes, too, have always had their defenders.

Lastly, some simply attribute the demise of the dinosaurs to lack of space on Noah's ark, the will of God, or even destructive little green men from outer space – which suggests that something else has been threatened with extinction: the spirit of scientific inquiry.

## The field of scientifically viable contenders has been narrowed

To their credit, these next hypotheses are comprehensive in that they attempt to account for all Late

Devastating volcanic eruptions and a comet or asteroid striking the earth figure prominently among the causes most recently proposed to explain the great dying of the Mesozoic. Extrapolated to a worldwide scale, the torrents of fire and lava spewed out by volcanoes (above, Mt Etna) would have had apocalyptic biological consequences. The catastrophic effects resulting from the impact of a comet or asteroid (Halley's Comet, far right) can only be imagined.

Mesozoic extinctions, not just the disappearance of the dinosaurs. Moreover, they are all predicated on the interpretation, however debatable, of scientific fact.

Recent general interest in astrophysics has fuelled speculation that an asteroid collided with the earth. When Walter Alvarez (University of California at Berkeley) and his crew discovered an iridium-rich layer in sediments that marked the boundary between the Cretaceous and the Tertiary, they proposed this theory based on the fact that the element iridium is far more abundant in material of extraterrestrial origin than on our own planet. The impact of a large comet nucleus or asteroid smashing into our planet would have thrown up huge amounts of dust, blocking out sunlight for several months and stopping all

Symbolizing the end of their eons-long wait, the little mammals in Mark Hallett's *Dawn of a New Day* have taken over a *Triceratops* skeleton and clambered onto its neck frill to survey the world they are about to conquer. But were they responsible for the decline and extinction of the mighty reptiles of the Mesozoic, as some maintain? This hypothesis is highly improbable. What the mammals actually did was to take advantage of opportunities the extinction of the dinosaurs created for them; they filled ecological niches left empty at the dawn of the Tertiary.

photosynthesis. This, in turn, would have triggered a disruption in the food chain and doomed certain animals, including dinosaurs.

Not all scientists subscribe to this view. We know of other iridium-rich layers that have no apparent connection with mass extinctions. Nor does this catastrophe theory account for the fact that many ecologically sensitive zoological groups managed to cling to life.

The second hypothesis, likewise recent, proposes much the same scenario, only with a different and simpler cause. According to some researchers, the high concentration of iridium in certain geological deposits was the result of intense volcanic activity.

Could the last dinosaur have been this ankylosaur that expired at the foot of a sequoia tree after a protracted death agony? Behind this seemingly frivolous question lies a fundamental issue. Some palaeontologists speculate that the extinction of the dinosaurs and the other groups that died out when they did spanned a period of one or perhaps as much as two or three million years.

They point to basalt formations in the Deccan Plateau of India, which date from the Cretaceous-Tertiary boundary, as evidence of this 'gradual' catastrophe. The expulsion of significant amounts of volcanic dust and the subsequent darkening of the skies would have had the same effects on flora and fauna, only without the suddenness of a collision.

Once again, certain geological and palaeontological data do not fit in with this hypothesis; confirming or disproving it will take years of investigation.

## The great retreat of Cretaceous seas

Another theory, proposed in 1964 by Léonard Ginsburg of the National Museum of Natural History

This timespan is roughly equivalent to the period between the appearance of the earliest hominid and modern *Homo sapiens*. Other theorists believe the great extinction may have taken only a few decades. As with everything pertaining to the history of life, the time factor is difficult to gauge and necessitates challenging adjustments in the way we think.

in Paris, is based on an acknowledged worldwide geological occurrence: the great retreat of the seas during the Late Cretaceous.

Although changes in the coastline, whether by retreating or encroaching water, were by no means unusual during the earth's history, what made the event at the end of the Mesozoic different was its phenomenal scope. Retreating seas may have exposed a substantial part of the continental plateau – as much as 200 metres in from the coast – and eventually killed off many marine organisms that were unaccustomed to the new habitat.

The new continental climate, with its seasonal fluctuations and more sharply contrasting day and night temperatures, would have had lethal consequences for large, cold-blooded animals like dinosaurs and even pterosaurs, but would have allowed small reptiles, crocodiles (with their specialized anatomy) and warm-blooded animals to survive. Some feel this hypothesis is the simplest and most inherently reliable, despite some admitted gaps.

### It's not how they died, but how they lived

Actually, not that many dinosaur specialists are interested in their extinction, for at least two reasons. For one thing, the phenomenon was not peculiar to dinosaurs. For another, we have a long way to go in understanding how they lived before we try to explain how they died.

What were dinosaurs? Animals whose magnificent 150-million-year flowering will continue to puzzle many a palaeontologist for generations to come.

This Eleanor Kish painting, *Chasmosaurus*, is suitably bleak. Overleaf: an 1883 engraving depicting the eruption of poisonous hot springs.

A. Bernard.

# DOCUMENTS

Dinosaurs left their mark around the world
in literature, comics and the movies

# How to find a dinosaur

*For many of us, our earliest, most vivid memory of a dinosaur comes from a visit to a science or natural history museum. But these spectacular skeletons didn't just walk into museums. How did they get there?*

Cope, Marsh and the other dinosaur hunters did not simply pick up dinosaur bones off the ground. Quite the opposite: the palaeontologist's job often begins with a long, tedious search through harsh, even dangerous, terrain in hope of finding even a single scrap of bone that will reveal the hidden presence of a trove of fossils.

In general, dinosaur fossils are far underground, buried by millions of years of accumulating earth and rock. Obviously, digging hundreds of feet in search of fossils is brutal, expensive, time-consuming work, without any guarantees of success. If all dinosaur fossils lay so entombed, we'd never have found out that the great reptiles existed.

Luckily, many of the fossils are not too hard to find. In many areas, such as the wind-whipped badlands of Montana and Alberta, canyons carved by rivers, and the deserts of Asia and Africa, the earth has been eroding for hundreds, or even thousands, of years, exposing rock that originally formed during the era of the dinosaurs. Elsewhere, rock quarries and road construction bring these rock strata to the surface far more quickly.

Many of these areas are rich in fossil bones and other mementos of the long-vanished reign of the dinosaurs. In some, teeth or scraps of bone may even have eroded entirely out of the earth, and may be found lying loose on the ground. Far more important fossils, however, are likely still to be ensconced in the rock below the surface.

Even after they've found evidence that a dinosaur skeleton or other fossils lie hidden – for example, a single large bone protruding from a rock face – the palaeontologists won't immediately begin digging. First, they will check

the area for additional fossil scraps, and will make careful note of the site's surroundings and location.

Then, with extreme care, the scientists will use shovels, pneumatic drills, or even carefully controlled explosives to remove the earth and rock that cover the fossilized bones. When only a few inches of rock remain, the process becomes far more painstaking; the collectors may spend days using tiny picks, delicate chisels and soft brushes to remove the last bits of rock without damaging the underlying bones.

The collectors will attempt to expose whatever bones lie in the fossil bed. This allows them to record, either in sketches or photographs, exactly where every bone was placed, essential information for determining the skeleton's original position.

Next comes the all-important process of removing the bones from the surrounding rock. This is the most risky and frightening part of the entire job. Every palaeontologist has seen weeks of effort dissolve into disaster, as an invaluable bone crumbles into dust as it's being taken from the rock.

Before beginning, the palaeontologists will dig deep trenches around every bone or accumulation of bones, leaving the fossils looking like monuments rising from the surrounding rock. Particularly soft and crumbly fossils may be sprayed or painted with a hardener, a resin that doesn't harm the bones but makes it less likely that they'll be damaged or destroyed during transport.

The collectors then encase the exposed surface of nearly every fossil with bandages soaked in plaster, which will further protect the bones during transport. When the plaster has dried, the palaeontologists will carefully dig

On these and the previous pages, scientists around the world can be seen finding and unearthing dinosaur bones and preparing them for transport.

beneath each fossil, eventually dislodging it from the rock. Then – and this is another terrifying moment – the fossil will be slowly and carefully turned over. Loose rock will be cleared away, the newly exposed side will also be plastered, and the fossil will finally be ready for transport.

Once a group of fossils has reached the museum, the plaster will be removed. Soft bones may receive an additional hardening, while all fossils are cleaned with more care than they could receive in the field. Narrow layers

or fragments of rock lying in hard-to-reach areas on delicate fossils are removed with precision tools, including electrical drills and needles that work in conjunction with a microscope. Weak acids that remove the rock but leave the fossilized bone are also employed.

Once the bones are in the best shape they can be, an expert palaeontologist enters the scene. If the type of dinosaur has not yet been identified, then the expert will study the bones, compare them to others previously collected, and attempt to make an identification.

Usually, though, the palaeontologist who first dug the bones will have identified the dinosaur.

Next, the expert will seek to identify each bone and determine its position on the skeleton. (The location of the bones at the site where they were collected is often of no use, as dinosaur fossil skeletons are usually jumbled and incomplete when they're first found.) A combination of logic and previously studied skeletons of similar dinosaurs provides a guide during reconstruction.

Very few dinosaur skeletons are found complete; much more often, a large number of important bones are missing. Again, using logic and previously reconstructed skeletons, the expert will build models of the missing bones or parts of bones, using fibreglass or plaster. Then the entire skeleton will be mounted in a lifelike pose on a metal or fibreglass frame, producing the massive, stunning skeletons that make the dinosaurs seem so real to us.

But reconstruction of the skeleton isn't the only work that scientists do back at the museum or laboratory. The dinosaur's posture, the size of its skull, the length of its limbs and other

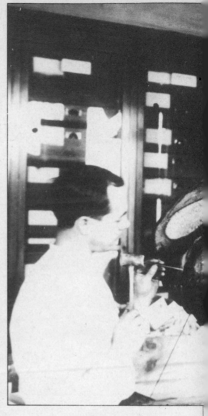

Once the bones make it back to the laboratory, there's still plenty of work to be done.

features can all help scientists gain important insights into the life, habits and death of the dinosaur being studied.

The reconstructed skeleton will obviously provide details about the dinosaur's size and weight. The length and shape of its limbs will indicate whether it ran on two feet, lumbered on four, or alternated between the two modes of locomotion. The shape of its feet may show the type of terrain it was best suited to, while the size of its eye sockets may give hints as to whether it

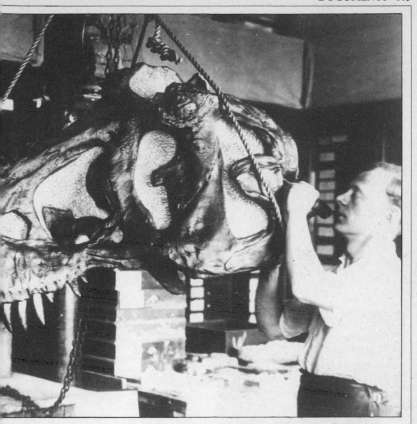

was active in dark forests or open prairies, at midday or at dusk.

A few times in the history of fossil hunting, palaeontologists have found the contents of a dinosaur's stomach fossilized along with the dinosaur itself. Far more often, though, the palaeontologist must determine a dinosaur's diet by studying its jaws. For example, duck-billed dinosaurs had no teeth in the front of the mouth but hundreds of flat teeth at the back, perfectly designed for grinding the coarse, fibrous vegetation that these dinosaurs ate. Similarly, the daggerlike teeth lining the powerful jaws of an *Albertosaurus* mark that carnosaur as an eater of meat.

With these and other insights, today's palaeontologists are able to do far more than reconstruct dinosaur skeletons. They can re-create a long-lost world in all its diversity and beauty, and place living, breathing dinosaurs in the centre of that world.

Joseph Wallace

# Expedition to the Gobi

*When Roy Chapman Andrews led an American Museum of Natural History expedition to the Gobi in 1919, one object was to have fun – which they did. But they also made some tremendous discoveries.*

Dinosaur footprint, Niger.

*Before setting out, Andrews made his intentions perfectly clear.*

**Gobi expedition of 1919 – plans and specifications**

OBJECT
To get to Urga eventually

MOTTO
'We should worry'

PERSONNEL
Mr R. C. Andrews – 'Gobi'
  Head cook, skinner, butcher, and general camp arranger and grouch
Mrs – ditto – 'Gobina'
  Photographess, assistant cook, meal and table arrangements
Mr Mac Callie, alias 'Delco'
  Chief electrician, tent pegger, water purveyor, and woodcutter
Mrs Mac Callie 'Delcette'
  Coffee, tea, and soup supply, chief table linen and cutlery
Mr C. L. Coltman 'Boss'
  Motor Engineer, time keeper, expert, and general commander
Mrs – ditto – 'Bossens'
  Assistant cook, quartermastress, finder of lost articles
Mr Owen 'Uncle John'
  Assistant motor engineer and all round help-less

REGULATIONS
1. No cussing the weather.
2. No insinuations if there is sand in the soup.
3. No grouching against the gasoline in the drinking water.
4. No profanity unless of picturesque variety.
5. All hands assist at unpacking and

packing in both the evening and the morning stops and starts.

6. All male members must take share in pumping tires and other work requiring more than hot air.

7. Camps will be made, starts made, stops made, and such disarrangements by vote, four votes carrying the day.

8. Any breach of regulations will be considered by court after dinner and during smoking hour (when most lenient judgment can be hoped for) and penalty judged will be walked by the culprit in miles recorded by speedometer at the start of the following day.

9. If male members of expedition cannot supply fresh meat on any one day they will not be allowed to smoke after dinner.

PLANS

1. To have a thoroughly good time.

2. To get good specimens of all game available.

3. Camp early and start late on general principle.

4. To stop and investigate, or leave the road and explore whenever desired.

The Grouchless Gang

*With their plans clearly stated, the 'gang' set out. The expedition proved astonishingly successful. Team members unearthed a great number of new dinosaurs (and some ancient mammals). Roy Chapman Andrews recorded some of the highlights in his journal (below).*

### Food and shelter

Ninety-nine out of every hundred persons think that hardships are an essential part of every explorer's existence. But I don't believe in hardships; they are a great nuisance. Eat well, dress well, sleep well, whenever it is possible is a pretty good rule for everyday use. Don't *court* hardships. Then you can work hard and steadily and if a bit of 'hardship' does come along in the course of things, you are ready to take it in your stride and laugh while it is going on. If you ask the members of the Central Asiatic Expedition about their hardships they will laugh at you. We seldom had any, and yet we were exploring a desert where there was virtually nothing to be obtained to eat except meat. We had twenty-six men in the field for two years and no illness. Could you equal that in New York?

All the equipment for the expedition with the exception of food and tents I purchased in New York. In the eighteen tons which were sent to Peking we had every modern invention for camp comfort. Because it is impossible to get vegetables of any kind in the Gobi I brought a quantity of dried onions, tomatoes, carrots, spinach, and beets from America, but all the other food was obtained from the American Legation Marine Corps Detachment through the courtesy of Colonel H. Dunlap and Lt Colonel Seth Williams.

We used Mongol tents and fur sleeping bags. Almost all explorers find that the natives have devised the best dwellings and the best clothes for their particular country and the conditions of life which it involves. The Mongols are no exception to this rule. They are nomads who are constantly moving as they follow their flocks or the dictates of their restless spirits. A permanent dwelling would be of little use for the grazing may be good at a certain place one year, but poor the next. Wind and cold are the most serious weather conditions to be met, they need not be worried about rain for even in the grasslands this seldom comes. Therefore, the tent which will stand against almost any Mongolian wind storm is made of durable cotton cloth, light in weight, but is not particularly waterproof.

## The first dinosaur ever discovered in Asia north of the Himalaya Mountains

While my wife and I were watching a sunset, which splashed the sky with gold and red, the last two cars swung around a brown earth bank and roared into camp. We went out to meet them. I knew something unusual had happened, for no one said a word. Granger's eyes were shining and he was puffing violently at a very odious pipe. So I supposed that the 'something' was good news.

Silently he dug into his pocket and produced a handful of bone fragments; out of his shirt came a rhinoceros tooth, and the various folds of his upper garments yielded other fossils. Berkey and Morris were loaded in a like manner. Granger held out his hand and said: 'Well, Roy, we've done it. The stuff is here. We picked up fifty pounds of bone in an hour.'

Then we all laughed and shouted and shook hands and pounded one another on the back and did all the things men do when they are very happy. No prospector ever examined the washings of a gold-pan with greater interest than we handled the little heap of fossil bones. Rhinoceroses we were sure of, and there were teeth that could only belong to the titanothere, a great

rhinoceros-like beast that became extinct long before the Age of Man. But no titanotheres had been discovered outside America, with the possible exception of a doubtful fragment from Austria! The other specimens were smaller mammals not positively identifiable, but we discussed and rediscussed the possible origin of every piece of bone. While dinner was being prepared, Granger wandered off along the grey-white outcrop that lay like a recumbent reptile west of camp. Even in the falling light, he discovered a half-dozen fossil bits. We realized that we had a new deposit at our very door.

We were all so eager for the next day's work that sleep came slowly and the camp was astir shortly after daylight. Before breakfast my wife and I walked out to inspect a line of traps that had been set in the sandy mounds of the basin floor. We had caught an interesting specimen of a new sand rat (*Meriones*), several large hamsters (*Cricetulus*), and a half-dozen kangaroo-rats (*Dipus*); all species new to my collection. While we were busy at the traps, we saw Dr Berkey with head bent and hands behind his back, wandering about on the ridge near camp. Soon he came in to breakfast with both hands filled with fossils. Granger examined them with a puzzled expression.

'For the life of me,' he said, 'I cannot make that anything but reptile. It might possibly be bird, but it must have been *some* bird to have a leg-bone like that. It certainly isn't mammalian.'

It was about two-thirds of one of the lower leg-bones which he held out. It had been found just above camp. A little

Removing dinosaur bones.

later, when Dr Black was walking to his tent, he almost stepped on the missing section, which made the specimen complete. It had obviously weathered out and rolled down from the ridge above. We were confident then that it was reptilian. The geologists, with Granger and Black, went up to the ridge where Dr Berkey found the bones. Just as my wife and I were starting out on a little shooting-trip, we met Dr Berkey on his way into camp. 'Come up with me,' he said; 'we've made a discovery, and a very important one.'

He would give us no more information until we reached the summit of the outcrop. Then he pointed to Granger, who was on his knees, working at something with a camel's-hair brush. 'Take a look at that and see what you make of it,' he said.

I saw a great bone beautifully preserved and outlined in the rock. There was no doubt this time; it was reptilian and, moreover, *dinosaur*.

'It means,' said Dr Berkey, 'that we are standing on Cretaceous strata of the upper part of the Age of Reptiles – *the first Cretaceous strata, and the first dinosaur ever discovered in Asia north of the Himalaya Mountains.*'

### Finding fossils

The method of finding fossils seems to be a mystery to the layman. As a matter of fact, it is merely a question of scientific knowledge and training. In the first place, geological conditions must be right. Volcanic and metamorphic rocks can never contain fossils; for they have been subjected to heat and chance, which destroy bones instead of preserving them. Thus fossils can occur only in sedimentary strata, such as sandstone, shale, and limestone. Fossils are being made today just as they were a million years ago. When an animal dies the skeleton may be covered with sand or other sediments. This heaps up higher and higher and eventually is consolidated into rock. Then a very slow change begins. Cell by cell the animal substance in the bone is replaced by mineral matter and the skeleton becomes petrified, or changed to stone. Sedimentary strata must not be too old – that is, they must not have been laid down before vertebrate animals existed – or naturally they cannot contain the bones of such animals. Not only must a region have the proper age and geological formation for fossils; it must also be opened and cut by ravines and gullies or have bluffs and ridges that give a cross-section through its structure.

Long before the Iren Dabasu basin was reached, we had been driving across

Camasaur skeleton.

sedimentary strata, but because they were not dissected there was little possibility of finding fossils. As soon as Berkey, Morris, and Granger saw the bluffs which we descended to the salt-lake flood-plain, they realized that here was what they had been seeking – a deeply exposed cross-section of the rock and sediment on the top of which we had been running for so many miles. From that moment it was simply a question of using their eyes to find bones that had been uncovered by the action of wind and rain.

Contrary to the general impression, a paleontologist seldom digs for fossils unless he sees them. Perhaps it is only the tiniest part of a bone that catches his trained eyes, but it may give the clue to the discovery of an entire skeleton. Perhaps the fossils lie completely exposed upon the surface or have been washed by rain or streams far away from the spot where they were originally buried. Berkey found the first dinosaur bone on the summit of the outcrop above camp. Black found the remaining fragment at the base of the exposure; evidently it had been washed down by a flood of rain, possibly not many days before we arrived. The long ridge beside which our tents were pitched contained bones, teeth, and claws of large and small flesh-eating and herbivorous dinosaurs.

### 'Our greatest find'

The evening of the geologists' return was exciting enough to keep me awake long after the lights were out, but the next was still more memorable. Late in the afternoon there was a little rain and just at sunset a glorious rainbow stretched its fairy arch from the plain across the lake to the summit of Baga

Bogdo. Below it the sky was ablaze with ragged tongues of flame; in the west billowy, gold-margined clouds, shot through with red, lay thick upon the desert. Wave after wave of light flooded the mountain across the lake – lavender, green, and deepest purple – colors which blazed and faded almost before they could be named. We exclaimed breathlessly at first and then grew silent with awe. We felt that we should never see the like again. Suddenly a black car, with Granger and Shackelford in it, came out of the north and slipped quietly into camp. Even Shackelford's buoyant spirit was stilled by the grandeur of what was passing in the sky. Not until the purple twilight had settled over the mountain, lake and desert, did the two men tell us why they had been so late. They had discovered parts of the skeleton of a *Baluchitherium* [a prehistoric mammal]!

During the entire Mongolian expedition the best localities for fossils and the finest specimens were discovered when we were on the point of leaving a region for other fields. So it was with our greatest find, the *Baluchitherium*. On breaking camp Granger and Shackelford decided to walk through a still uninspected pocket in the bad lands and to have Wang, their Chinese chauffeur, drive their car ahead to a promontory two miles to the south. After a little, Wang, bored with waiting for them, decided to do some prospecting on his own account. Almost immediately he discovered a huge bone in the bottom of a gully that emptied into a ravine. Full of excitement, he climbed back into the car, and, when Granger and Shackelford arrived, proudly conducted

Camasaur cranium, still embedded in rock.

them to the spot where he had found the fossil.

It was the end of the humerus, or upper fore leg-bone, of a *Baluchitherium*, and other parts were visible, partially embedded in the earth. The most important of all was one whole side of the lower jaw.

The bones were very well preserved and the men removed without difficulty all that they could discover. They searched the sides of the gully until the approaching sunset warned them to be on the way to Tsagan Nor if they wished to reach camp before dark....

No newborn baby ever was handled with more loving care than we bestowed upon those precious bones as we packed them in coats and bags, so that they would ride safely.

At six o'clock, while the men were having tea, we burst into camp, shouting like children. Granger has made so many interesting discoveries in his paleontological career that he is not easily stirred, but our story brought him up standing. Then silently and carefully he inspected the bones in the car.

We held a council over the largest of them, which was partly embedded in rock. It was difficult to identify at first; for we were dealing with an animal virtually unknown. At last Granger

On a 1973 expedition to the Ténéré Desert, Niger, a team made this remarkable find.

decided that the bone was the front of the skull. Then we made out two great incisor teeth and the bones of the maxillae and premaxillae. There was no doubt that we had also the posterior part of the skull; for I had identified the great occipital condyles and the neural canal, through which runs the spinal cord. Even though we had realized that the *Baluchitherium* was a colossal beast, the size of the bones left us absolutely astounded. The largest known rhinoceros was dwarfed in comparison; for the head of this animal

was five feet long and his neck must have been of pillar-like proportions.

Early in the morning Colgate, Granger, Shackelford, Wang, and I set merrily forth in one of the Fulton trucks for the scene of the great find. Shackelford and Walter lay back in camp-chairs, singing at the top of their voices. I suppose that fossils never were collected under happier circumstances.

When we arrived at the bottom of the gully, Granger and I made a careful examination of the skull. We decided that it was lying on its right side and that the left arch and tooth-row were gone. Later we found these conjectures to be correct.

Granger, Wang, and I sifted every inch of the sand and gravel in the bottom of the wash, salvaging bits of bone and teeth. Granger carefully worked around the skull itself. While he whisked out the sand, grain by grain, the rest of us scattered over the surrounding bad lands to see if we could locate other bones. The skeleton had evidently lain near the summit of a

ridge left between two gullies and had broken up as the earth weathered away and heavy rains fell. Part of it had gone down one side of the slope; this was what Wang had found the first day. The rest had rolled into the main wash, where I discovered it. And now Shackelford picked up a half-dozen important skull fragments, out on the plain at least three hundred yards from the ravine.

It took Granger four days to remove the skull; for it had to be encased in a shell of burlap and paste for safe transit by motor, camel, railroad, and steamship, to New York.

In the meantime we made several short excursions. But it was already August 9 and, although the weather was still hot, geese and ducks were flocking and sand-grouse were flying eastward in countless thousands. I did not need these signs to tell me that winter was approaching and that it was time for us to take the trail. Yet we could not leave until we had spent a day at a grey bluff across the lake where Berkey and Morris had found Pliocene fossils. Cars could not possibly cross the sand-dunes; so on August 10 we set forth on camels.

The next afternoon the other men found some fine things in the grey beds, but I had the best luck of all. While inspecting a knoll of yellow gravel, I noticed a few fossil bits at the very base. Following them up, I came to a slight discoloration in the earth and saw a half-inch of bone exposed. Since I had found the calcaneum of a mastodon a few moments earlier, I thought that this was the end of a tusk, which very likely was fastened into the skull of a proboscidean. I scraped away the earth and soon realized that the fossil was not an elephant's tusk, but the antler of a

stag – as perfect as if it had been dropped the day before instead of nearly a million years ago. I had long been interested in the living Asiatic wapiti because of its relationship to the elk of western America and to the red deer of Europe, and it was probable that in this very fossil we might have the ancestor of them both.

The actual removing of the antler was too delicate an undertaking for my pick-and-shovel methods; so I walked to the end of the knoll and fired three shots with my automatic pistol to bring up Granger and Shackelford, who, I knew, were somewhere in the maze of gullies below me. Before long they appeared, hot and puffing; for among the members of the Expedition such a signal meant that every man within hearing distance should not stand upon the order of his coming, but come as fast as his legs could carry him. Though it was then six o'clock, Granger was able to paste the antler with gum arabic and rice-paper and remove it.

As the sun was setting, we started for the long ride to camp. Before we had entered the dunes, darkness had fallen and a strong wind blew from the east. We urged our camels to their best speed; for it would have been decidedly dangerous to become lost in that drifting maze when a sandstorm was in progress. But before we left the last of the fantastic waves behind us, the wind dropped as suddenly as it had risen, the thickly piled clouds on the horizon disappeared and a glorious moon lighted us home.

A lso from the Ténéré Desert (opposite): a dinosaur rib (above), dinosaur shoulder blade (left), and a crocodile tooth (right).

# Dinosaurs in fiction

*Dinosaurs and their world still capture the imagination of novelists... and their readers.*

Tyrannosaurus – even more awful in our imagination than it was in reality?

## Voyage to the past

We were all sleeping round our dying fire when we were aroused – or, rather, I should say, shot out of our slumbers – by a succession of the most frightful cries and screams to which I have ever listened. I know no sound to which I could compare this amazing tumult, which seemed to come from some spot within a few hundred yards of our camp. It was as ear-splitting as any whistle of a railway-engine; but whereas the whistle is a clear, mechanical, sharp-edged sound, this was far deeper in volume and vibrant with the uttermost strain of agony and horror. We clapped our hands to our ears to shut out that nerve-shaking appeal. A cold sweat broke out over my body, and my heart turned sick at the misery of it. All the woes of tortured life, all its stupendous indictment of high heaven, its innumerable sorrows, seemed to be centred and condensed into that one dreadful, agonized cry. And then, under this high-pitched, ringing sound there was another, more intermittent, a low, deep-chested laugh, a growling, throaty gurgle of merriment which formed a grotesque accompaniment to the shriek with which it was blended. For three or four minutes on end the fearsome duet continued, while all the foliage rustled with the rising of startled birds. Then it shut off as suddenly as it began. For a long time we sat in horrified silence. Then Lord John threw a bundle of twigs upon the fire, and their red glare lit up the intent faces of my companions and flickered over the great boughs above our heads.

'What was it?' I whispered.

'We shall know in the morning,' said

Lord John. 'It was close to us – not farther than the glade.'

'We have been privileged to overhear a prehistoric tragedy, the sort of drama which occurred among the reeds upon the border of some Jurassic lagoon, when the greater dragon pinned the lesser among the slime,' said Challenger, with more solemnity than I had ever heard in his voice. 'It was surely well for man that he came late in the order of creation. There were powers abroad in earlier days which no courage and no mechanism of his could have met. What could his sling, his throwing-stick, or his arrow avail him against such forces as have been loose to-night? Even with a modern rifle it would be all odds on the monster.'

'I think I should back my little friend,' said Lord John, caressing his Express. 'But the beast would certainly have a good sporting chance.'

Summerlee raised his hand.

'Hush!' he cried. 'Surely I hear something?'

From the utter silence there emerged a deep, regular pat-pat. It was the tread of some animal – the rhythm of soft but heavy pads placed cautiously upon the ground. It stole slowly round the camp, and then halted near our gateway. There was a low, sibilant rise and fall – the breathing of the creature. Only our feeble hedge separated us from this horror of the night. Each of us had seized his rifle, and Lord John had pulled out a small bush to make an embrasure in the hedge.

'By George!' he whispered. 'I think I can see it!'

I stooped and peered over his shoulder through the gap. Yes, I could see it, too. In the deep shadow of the tree there was a deeper shadow yet, black, inchoate, vague – a crouching form full of savage vigour and menace. It was no higher than a horse, but the dim outline suggested vast bulk and strength. That hissing pant, as regular and full-volumed as the exhaust of an engine, spoke of a monstrous organism. Once, as it moved, I thought I saw the glint of two terrible, greenish eyes. There was an uneasy rustling, as if it were crawling slowly forward.

'I believe it is going to spring!' said I, cocking my rifle.

'Don't fire! Don't fire!' whispered Lord John. 'The crash of a gun in this silent night would be heard for miles. Keep it as a last card.'

'If it gets over the hedge we're done,' said Summerlee, and his voice crackled into a nervous laugh as he spoke.

'No, it must not get over,' cried Lord John; 'but hold your fire to the last. Perhaps I can make something of the fellow. I'll chance it, anyhow.'

It was as brave an act as ever I saw a man do. He stooped to the fire, picked up a blazing branch, and slipped in an instant through a sallyport which he had made in our gateway. The thing moved forward with a dreadful snarl. Lord John never hesitated, but, running towards it with a quick, light step, he dashed the flaming wood into the brute's face. For one moment I had a vision of a horrible mask like a giant toad's, of a warty, leprous skin, and of a loose mouth all beslobbered with fresh blood. The next, there was a crash in the underwood and our dreadful visitor was gone.

'I thought he wouldn't face the fire,' said Lord John, laughing, as he threw his branch among the faggots.

'You should not have taken such a risk!' we all cried.

'There was nothin' else to be done. If he had got among us we should have shot each other in tryin' to down him. On the other hand, if we had fired through the hedge and wounded him he would soon have been on the top of us – to say nothin' of giving ourselves away. On the whole, I think that we are jolly well out of it. What was he, then?'

Our learned men looked at each other with some hesitation.

'Personally, I am unable to classify the creature with any certainty,' said Summerlee, lighting his pipe from the fire.

'In refusing to commit yourself you are but showing a proper scientific reserve,' said Challenger, with massive condescension. 'I am not myself prepared to go farther than to say in general terms that we have almost certainly been in contact to-night with some form of carnivorous dinosaur. I have already expressed my anticipation that something of the sort might exist upon this plateau.'

'We have to bear in mind,' remarked Summerlee, 'that there are many prehistoric forms which have never come down to us. It would be rash to suppose that we can give a name to all that we are likely to meet.'

'Exactly. A rough classification may be the best that we can attempt. To-morrow some further evidence may help us to an identification. Meantime we can only renew our interrupted slumbers.'

It was a fearsome walk, and one which will be with me so long as memory holds. In the great moonlight clearings I slunk along among the shadows on the margin. In the jungle I crept forward, stopping with a beating heart whenever I heard, as I often did, the crash of breaking branches as some wild beast went past. Now and then great shadows loomed up for an instant and were gone – great, silent shadows which seemed to prowl upon padded feet. How often I stopped with the intention of returning, and yet every time my pride conquered my fear, and sent me on again until my object should be obtained.

At last (my watch showed that it was one in the morning) I saw the gleam of water amid the openings of the jungle, and ten minutes later I was among the reeds upon the borders of the central lake. I was exceedingly dry, so I lay down and took a long draught of its waters, which were fresh and cold. There was a broad pathway with many tracks upon it at the spot which I had found, so that it was clearly one of the drinking-places of the animals. Close to the water's edge there was a huge isolated block of lava. Up this I climbed, and, lying on the top, I had an excellent view in every direction.

The first thing which I saw filled me with amazement. When I described the view from the summit of the great tree, I said that on the farther cliff I could see a number of dark spots, which appeared to be the mouths of caves. Now, as I looked up at the same cliffs, I saw discs of light in every direction, ruddy, clearly defined patches, like the port-holes of a liner in the darkness. For a moment I thought it was the lava-glow from some volcanic action; but this could not be so. Any volcanic action would surely be down in the hollow, and not high among the rocks. What, then, was the alternative? It was wonderful, and yet it

A nother vision: woodcut from an 1886 French book by Camille Flammarion, *The World Before the Creation of Man.*

must surely be. These ruddy spots must be the reflection of fires within the caves – fires which could only be lit by the hand of man. There were human beings, then, upon the plateau. How gloriously my expedition was justified! Here was news indeed for us to bear back with us to London!

For a long time I lay and watched these red, quivering blotches of light. I suppose they were ten miles off from me, yet even at that distance one could observe how, from time to time, they twinkled or were obscured as someone passed before them. What would I not have given to be able to crawl up to them, to peep in, and to take back some word to my comrades as to the appearance and character of the race who lived in so strange a place! It was out of the question for the moment, and yet surely we could not leave the plateau until we had some definite knowledge upon the point.

Lake Gladys – my own lake – lay like a sheet of quicksilver before me, with a reflected moon shining brightly in the centre of it. It was shallow, for in many places I saw low sandbanks protruding above the water. Everywhere upon the still surface I could see signs of life, sometimes mere rings and ripples in the water, sometimes the gleam of a great silver-sided fish in the air, sometimes the arched, slate-coloured back of some passing monster. Once upon a yellow sandbank I saw a creature like a huge swan, with a clumsy body and a high, flexible neck, shuffling about upon the margin. Presently it plunged in, and for some time I could see the arched neck and darting head undulating over the water. Then it dived, and I saw it no more.

My attention was soon drawn away from these distant sights and brought back to what was going on at my very feet. Two creatures like large armadillos had come down to the drinking-place, and were squatting at the edge of the water, their long, flexible tongues like red ribbons shooting in and out as they lapped. A huge deer, with branching horns, a magnificent creature which carried itself like a king, came down with its doe and two fawns and drank beside the armadillos. No such deer exist anywhere else upon earth, for the

moose or elks which I have seen would hardly have reached its shoulders. Presently it gave a warning snort, and was off with its family among the reeds, while the armadillos also scuttled for shelter. A new-comer, a most monstrous animal, was coming down the path.

For a moment I wondered where I could have seen that ungainly shape, that arched back with triangular fringes along it, that strange bird-like head held close to the ground. Then it came back to me. It was the stegosaurus – the very creature which Maple White had preserved in his sketchbook, and which had been the first object which arrested the attention of Challenger! There he was – perhaps the very specimen which the American artist had encountered.

The ground shook beneath his tremendous weight, and his gulpings of water resounded through the still night. For five minutes he was so close to my rock that by stretching out my hand I could have touched the hideous waving hackles upon his back. Then he lumbered away and was lost among the boulders.

Looking at my watch, I saw that it was half-past two o'clock, and high time, therefore, that I started upon my homeward journey. There was no difficulty about the direction in which I should return, for all along I had kept the little brook upon my left, and it opened into the central lake within a stone's-throw of the boulder upon which I had been lying. I set off, therefore, in high spirits, for I felt that I had done good work and was bringing back a fine budget of news for my companions. Foremost of all, of course, were the sight of the fiery caves and the certainty that some troglodytic race inhabited them. But besides that I could speak from experience of the central lake. I could testify that it was full of strange creatures, and I had seen several land forms of primeval life which we had not before encountered. I reflected as I walked that few men in the world could have spent a stranger night or added more to human knowledge in the course of it.

I was plodding up the slope, turning these thoughts over in my mind, and had reached a point which may have been half-way to home, when my mind was brought back to my own position by a strange noise behind me. It was something between a snore and a growl,

A Mesozoic landscape as seen in an 1880 German watercolour.

low, deep, and exceedingly menacing. Some strange creature was evidently near me, but nothing could be seen, so I hastened more rapidly upon my way. I had traversed a half a mile or so when suddenly the sound was repeated, still behind me, but louder and more menacing than before. My heart stood still within me as it flashed across me that the beast, whatever it was, must surely be after *me*. My skin grew cold and my hair rose at the thought. That these monsters should tear each other to pieces was a part of the strange struggle for existence, but that they should turn upon modern man, that they should deliberately track and hunt down the predominant human, was a staggering and fearsome thought. I remembered again the blood-beslobbered face which we had seen in the glare of Lord John's torch, like some horrible vision from the deepest circle of Dante's hell. With my knees shaking beneath me, I stood and glared with starting eyes down the moonlit path which lay behind me. All was quiet as in a dream landscape. Silver clearings and the black patches of the bushes – nothing else could I see. Then from out of the silence, imminent and threatening, there came once more that low, throaty croaking, far louder and closer than before. There could no longer be a doubt. Something was on my trail, and was closing in upon me every minute.

I stood like a man paralyzed, still staring at the ground which I had traversed. Then suddenly I saw it. There was movement among the bushes at the far end of the clearing which I had just traversed. A great dark shadow disengaged itself and hopped out into the clear moonlight. I say 'hopped' advisedly, for the beast moved like a kangaroo, springing along in an erect position upon its powerful hind-legs, while its front ones were held bent in front of it. It was of enormous size and power, like an erect elephant, but its movements, in spite of its bulk, were exceedingly alert. For a moment, as I saw its shape, I hoped that it was an iguanodon, which I knew to be harmless, but, ignorant as I was, I soon saw that this was a very different creature. Instead of the gentle, deer-shaped head of the great three-toed leaf-eater, this beast had a broad, squat, toad-like face like that which had alarmed us in our camp. His ferocious cry and the horrible energy of his pursuit both assured me that this was surely one of the great flesh-eating dinosaurs, the most terrible beasts which have ever walked this earth. As the huge brute loped along it dropped forward upon its fore-paws and brought its nose to the ground every twenty yards or so. It was smelling out my trail. Sometimes, for an instant, it was at fault. Then it would catch it up again and come bounding swiftly along the path I had taken.

Even now when I think of that nightmare the sweat breaks out upon my brow. What could I do? My useless fowling-piece was in my hand. What help could I get from that? I looked desperately round for some rock or tree, but I was in a bushy jungle with nothing higher than a sapling within sight, while I knew that the creature behind me could tear down an ordinary tree as though it were a reed. My only possible chance lay in flight. I could not move swiftly over the rough, broken ground, but as I looked round me in despair I saw a well-marked, hard-beaten path which ran across in front of me. We had seen several of the sort, the runs of various wild beasts, during our expeditions. Along this I could perhaps hold my own, for I was a fast runner, and in excellent condition. Flinging away my useless gun, I set myself to do such a half-mile as I have never done before or since. My limbs ached, my chest heaved, I felt that my throat would burst for want of air, and yet with that horror behind me I ran and I ran and ran. At last I paused, hardly able to move. For a moment I thought that I had thrown him off. The path lay still behind me. And then suddenly, with a crashing and a rending, a thudding of giant feet and a panting of monster lungs the beast was upon me once more. He was at my very heels. I was lost.

Madman that I was to linger so long before I fled! Up to then he had hunted by scent, and his movement was slow. But he had actually seen me as I started to run. From then onwards he had hunted by sight, for the path showed him where I had gone. Now, as he came round the curve, he was springing in great bounds. The moonlight shone upon his huge projecting eyes, the row of enormous teeth in his open mouth, and the gleaming fringe of claws upon his short, powerful forearms. With a scream of terror I turned and rushed wildly down the path. Behind me the thick, gasping breathing of the creature sounded louder and louder. His heavy footfall was beside me. Every instant I expected to feel his grip upon my back. And then suddenly there came a crash – I was falling through space, and everything beyond was darkness and rest.

Sir Arthur Conan Doyle
*The Lost World*, 1912

## The unassailable logic of dinosaurs

Not until the afternoon, as they were coming down on to the plains, did they see the first creatures of the plains, sporting in a valley. Instinct asserting itself, Bush's impulse was to watch them from behind a tree. Then he recalled they were less than ghosts to these bulky creatures, and walked out into the open towards them. Ann followed.

Eighteen stegosauri seemed to fill the small valley. The male was a giant, perhaps twenty feet long and round as a barrel, his spiky armour making him appear much larger than he was. The chunky plates along his backbone were a dull slaty green, but much of his body armour was a livid orange. He tore at foliage with his jaws, but perpetually kept his beady eyes alert for danger.

He had two females with him. They were smaller than he, and more lightly armoured. One in particular was prettily marked, the plates of her spine being almost the same light yellow as her underbelly.

About the stegosauri frisked their young. Bush and Ann walked among them, absolutely immune. There were fifteen of them, and obviously not many weeks hatched. Unencumbered as yet by more than the lightest vestige of armour, they skipped about their mothers like lambs, often standing on their tall hind legs, sometimes jumping over their parents' wickedly spiked tails.

The two humans stood in the middle of the herd, watching the antics of the young reptiles.

'Maybe that's why these things became extinct,' Ann said. 'The young ones all got hooked on jumping their mothers' tails and spiked themselves to death!'

'It's as good as any other theory to date.'

Only then did he notice the intruder, although the old man stegosaur had been backing about puffily for some while. From a nearby thicket, another animal was watching the scene. Bush took Ann's arm and directed her attention to the spot. As he did so, the bushes parted and another stegosaurus emerged. This was a male, smaller and presumably younger than the leader of the herd, his tail swishing from side to side.

The females and the young paid only the most cursory attention to the intruder; the females continued to munch, the youngsters to play. The leader immediately charged forward to deal with the intruder; he was being challenged for the possession of the herd.

Travelling smartly towards each other, the two males hit, shoulder to shoulder. To the humans, it was entirely soundless. The two great beasts stood there absorbing the shock, and then slowly pressed forward until they were side by side, one facing one way, one the other. They began to heave at each other, using their tails for leverage but never as weapons. Their mouths opened. They displayed little sharp teeth. Still the females and their young showed no interest in what was happening.

The males strained and struggled, their legs bowed until their ungainly bodies almost touched the ground. The older animal was winning by sheer weight. Suddenly the intruder was forced to take a step backwards. The leader nearly fell onto him. They stood apart. For a moment, the intruder looked back at the females, his mouth

hanging open. Then he lumbered off into the nearby thicket and was not seen again.

After a few snorts of triumph, the leader of the little herd returned to his females. They looked up, then resumed their placid munching.

'A lot they care what happens to him!' Bush said.

'They've probably learned by now that there's not much to choose between one male and another.'

He looked sharply at her. She was grinning. He softened, and smiled back.

When they climbed out of the far end of the valley, they had a wide panorama of the plains with a river meandering through them. Great forests started again a mile or two away. Close at hand, situated on a long outcrop of rock, was the Borrows' tent, and other signs of human habitation.

2.

'At least we can get a drink,' Ann said as they approached the motley collection of tents.

'You go ahead. I want to stay here for a while and think.' Bush still had his head stuffed full of dinosaurs. They disturbed him. Morally? Two men fighting over women rarely showed as little vindictiveness as those great armoured vegetarians. Aesthetically? Who could say what beauty was, except from his own standpoint? In any case, that great spinal column, rising to its highest point over the pelvis and then dying away in the spiked tail, had its own unassailable logic.

Brian W. Aldiss
*Cryptozoic!*, 1967

# The lighter side

*Far from being extinct, dinosaurs thrive in the comics.*

Anyone who has children, or has ever met one, quickly finds out how much they know about dinosaurs. It seems that almost as soon as they can read, they can identify dinosaurs you've never heard of, and they begin spotting errors in dinosaur books, in magazine articles, even on stuffed animals, when you'd think they'd be too young even to pronounce 'palaeontologist'.

If kids have got something to say about dinosaurs, don't argue – they know what they're talking about. This fund of knowledge – and desire for accuracy – makes all the more surprising the ongoing lack of realistic comics and other illustrated material about dinosaurs. Too often, what does exist is either slipshod or egregiously wrong, featuring, for example, dinosaurs living side by side with cavemen. No child with any self-respect would believe that one.

Today, however, a pair of daily comic strips are treating children with the respect they deserve, as well as assuming a certain level of dinosaur knowledge among adults.

From Gary Larson's 'The Far Side'.

In his *Calvin and Hobbes* Bill Watterson clearly comprehends the deep appeal that dinosaurs have for six-year-old boys, while Gary Larson's *The Far Side* has achieved much renown for being the first comic to reveal the essential comedy at the heart of most scientific endeavours – including the study of dinosaurs.

Joseph Wallace

The real reason dinosaurs became extinct

"What a find, Williams! The fossilized footprint of a brachiosaurus!…And a Homo habilus thrown in to boot!"

"Most peculiar, Sidney…another scattering of cub scout attire."

Bill Watterson's Calvin lives in a world still populated with dinosaurs. They're a lot more entertaining than grown-ups.

# At the movies

*We might never have treated dinosaurs with the fascination they deserve if not for nearly eight decades of movies that have brought the long-extinct reptiles to life.*

As long ago as 1915, at the very dawn of the movie era, a man named Willis O'Brien unveiled the first fruits of a lifelong obsession with movie dinosaurs: *The Dinosaur and the Missing Link*. This five-minute movie featured clay dinosaurs animated through stop-motion; the models were moved a tiny bit from frame to frame. The result: dinosaurs that seemed alive onscreen.

The same technique informed O'Brien's 1919 *The Ghost of Slumber Mountain*, which depicted a contemporary hidden valley containing *Triceratops* and other dinosaurs. For the first time, a movie illustrated a profound hope that many amateur dinosaur-hunters still harbour: that somewhere, in the deepest wilderness, dinosaurs wait to be discovered.

*The Ghost of Slumber Mountain* was just the first of many movies to imagine that if we only searched hard enough, we'd find the dinosaurs themselves, not just their fossilized bones. None was more influential, however, than another O'Brien work: *The Lost World* (1925), based on Sir Arthur Conan Doyle's famous novel. Anyone who ever, as a child, saw the intrepid team of explorers encountering dinosaurs and cavemen in a South American mountain valley, dreamed for years of making such a discovery.

But Willis O'Brien was not done yet, and wasn't hampered by the advent of sound in movies in the late 1920s. In 1933, he unveiled one of the greatest special-effects movies in history: *King Kong*. Kong himself, of course, was a gigantic gorilla, but his island homeland was also populated with brilliantly animated dinosaurs.

Perhaps because O'Brien was so far

ahead of the field, no one stepped in to fill the gap when he stopped making dinosaur movies. Dinosaurs were in short supply, and those that did appear – such as the dinosaur skeleton being built by shy palaeontologist Cary Grant, only to be destroyed by wacky heiress Katharine Hepburn in 1937's *Bringing up Baby* – were used more as plot pegs than as subjects.

There were exceptions. Walt Disney's *Fantasia* (1940) featured a stunning (if inaccurate) segment with cartoon *Tyrannosaurus, Stegosaurus,* and other dinosaurs marching across a changing world to the strains of Stravinsky's 'Rite of Spring'. Far more embarrassing was 1940's *One Million BC,* which didn't even feature animated dinosaurs, but close-up footage of lizards with spines and horns strapped to their bodies.

The dinosaur movie began to make a comeback in the early 1950s. But in that paranoiac, atomic, Cold War era the dinosaurs were no longer confined to distant lost valleys or islands. Instead, these gigantic reptiles were far more likely to be roused by exposure to nuclear radiation, and, in response, to wreak death and destruction on even the world's largest and most impregnable cities.

One such classic revenge tale was 1953's *The Beast from 20,000 Fathoms,* in which an enormous carnosaur is riled by an atomic explosion, and takes out its anger on New York City. Seeing familiar bridges and other landmarks (not to mention countless people) destroyed by this out-for-blood beast was a chilling reminder of the world's vulnerability in the nuclear age.

But New York wasn't the only city targeted by outraged dinosaurs. In 1961's *Gorgo* a mother carnosaur

descended on London to rescue her baby. And, of course, the most frequent urban victim was Tokyo, repeatedly razed in the most ferocious manner possible by Godzilla, a nuclear-nightmare dinosaur that came equipped with radioactive breath.

With the dwindling of the 1950s' science-fiction boom came more lean times for the dinosaur movie. A few competent movies appeared subsequently, such as 1966's *One Million Years BC,* which featured Willis O'Brien-style stop-motion dinosaurs, as well as Raquel Welch in a skimpy loincloth. Other latter-day movies, including 1969's *Valley of the Gwangi* and 1975's woeful *The Land that Time Forgot,* were quite rightly ignored.

The 1980s saw very few dinosaur movies of any kind. Disney's *Baby: The Secret of the Lost Legend* (1985) took animation backward more than seventy years; Willis O'Brien would have been embarrassed to produce a dinosaur as stiff and lifeless as the young sauropod featured in this flop. 1988's animated *The Land Before Time* was better, though weighed down by overly cute baby dinosaurs.

In the 1990s movie special-effects technology has never been more advanced; technicians can virtually produce our wildest dreams onscreen. Maybe someday soon a talented team will create a dinosaur movie beyond our imaginings, one that will spur yet another generation's love affair with the dinosaurs.

Joseph Wallace

Scenes from *One Million Years BC* (pages 130-4), a 1966 look at the Mesozoic.

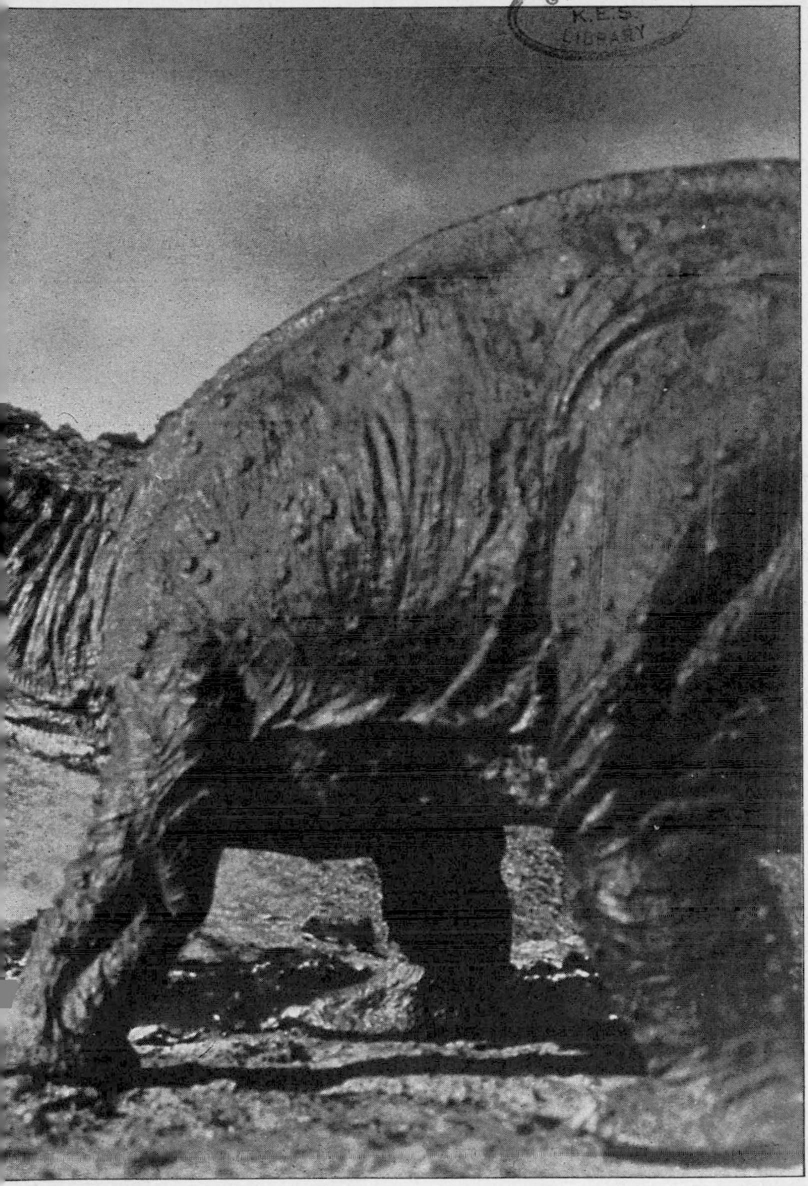

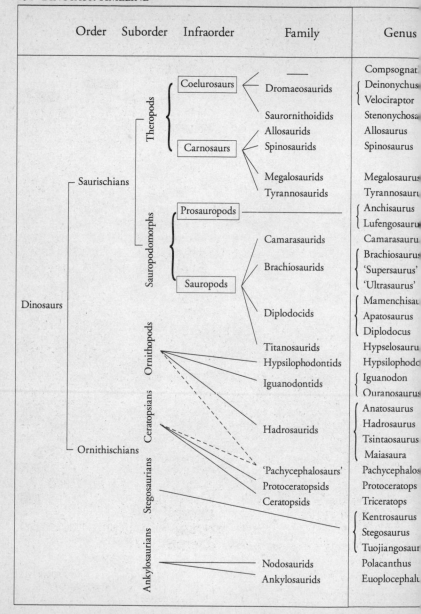

| Order | Suborder | Infraorder | Family | Genus |
|---|---|---|---|---|
| | | Coelurosaurs | — | Compsognat |
| | | | Dromaeosaurids | Deinonychus / Velociraptor |
| | | | Saurornithoidids | Stenonychosa |
| | | Carnosaurs | Allosaurids | Allosaurus |
| | | | Spinosaurids | Spinosaurus |
| | | | Megalosaurids | Megalosaurus |
| | | | Tyrannosaurids | Tyrannosauru |
| | | Prosauropods | — | Anchisaurus / Lufengosauru |
| | | | Camarasaurids | Camarasauru |
| | | | Brachiosaurids | Brachiosaurus / 'Supersaurus' / 'Ultrasaurus' |
| | | Sauropods | Diplodocids | Mamenchisau / Apatosaurus / Diplodocus |
| | | | Titanosaurids | Hypselosauru |
| | | | Hypsilophodontids | Hypsilophodo |
| | | | Iguanodontids | Iguanodon / Ouranosaurus |
| | | | Hadrosaurids | Anatosaurus / Hadrosaurus / Tsintaosaurus / Maiasaura |
| | | | 'Pachycephalosaurs' | Pachycephalos |
| | | | Protoceratopsids | Protoceratops |
| | | | Ceratopsids | Triceratops |
| | | | — | Kentrosaurus / Stegosaurus / Tuojiangosaur |
| | | | Nodosaurids | Polacanthus |
| | | | Ankylosaurids | Euoplocephalu |

Labels (vertical/left side): Dinosaurs; Saurischians; Ornithischians; Theropods; Sauropodomorphs; Ornithopods; Ceratopsians; Stegosaurians; Ankylosaurians

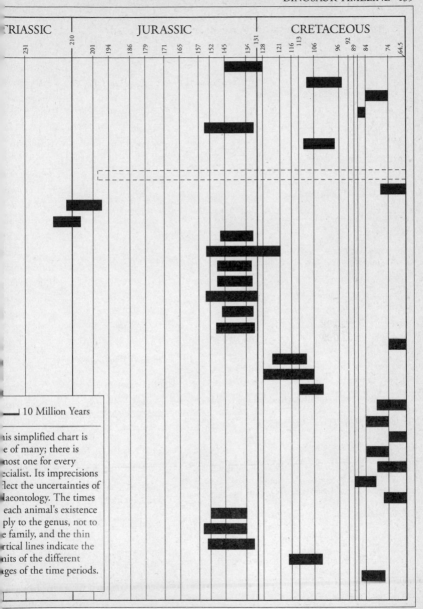

TRIASSIC | JURASSIC | CRETACEOUS

231 | 210 | 201 | 194 | 186 | 179 | 171 | 165 | 157 | 152 | 145 | 136 | 131 | 128 | 121 | 116 | 113 | 106 | 96 | 92 | 89 | 84 | 74 | 64.5

10 Million Years

This simplified chart is one of many; there is almost one for every specialist. Its imprecisions reflect the uncertainties of palaeontology. The times of each animal's existence apply to the genus, not to the family, and the thin vertical lines indicate the limits of the different ages of the time periods.

# FURTHER READING

Alexander, R. McNeil. *The Dynamics of Dinosaurs and Other Extinct Giants.* 1989·

Augusta, Joseph, and Zdeněk Burian. *Prehistoric Animals.* Trans. Dr Greta Horn. 1956

Bakker, Robert T. *The Dinosaur Heresies.* 1986

Benton, Michael. *Dinosaurs: An A-Z Guide.* 1988
—. *On the Trail of the Dinosaurs.* 1989

Bird, Roland T. *Bones for Barnum Brown: Adventures of a Dinosaur Hunter.* 1985

Bonaparte, J.-F., and E. H. Colbert et al. *Sulle orme dei dinosauri.* 1984

Brosnan, John. *Future Tense: The Cinema of Science Fiction.* 1978

Burton, Jane, and Dougal Dixon. *Time Exposure: A Photographic Record of the Dinosaur Age.* 1984

Casier, E. *Les Iguanodons de Bernissart.* 1978

Charig, Alan. *A New Look at the Dinosaurs.* 1979

Colbert, Edwin H. *The Great Dinosaur Hunters and Their Discoveries.* 1984

Desmond, A. J. *The Hot-Blooded Dinosaurs.* 1975

*Dinosaurs and Their Living Relatives.* 1985

*Dinosaurs Past and Present.* Vols. 1 and 2. 1987

Dixon, Dougal, Barry Cox, R. J. G. Savage and Brian Gardiner. *The Macmillan Illustrated Encyclopedia of Dinosaurs and Prehistoric Animals.* 1988

Dong Zhiming. *Dinosaurs from China.* 1988

Glut, Donald F. *The New Dinosaur Dictionary.* 1982

Hallam, A. *A Revolution in the Earth Sciences: from Continental Drift to Plate Tectonics.* 1973

Halstead, L. B. and Jenny. *Dinosaurs.* 1981

Horner, John R., and James Gorman. *Digging Dinosaurs.* 1988

Lambert, David. *Collins Guide to Dinosaurs.* 1983

Martin, Francine, and Pierre Bultynk. *The Iguanadons of Bernissart.* 1990

Mazin, J.-M. *Ce que l'On sait vraiment des dinosaures.* 1986

McLoughlin, John C. *Archosauria: A New Look at the Old Dinosaur.* 1979

Milner, Angela C. *Claws.* 1987

Norman, David. *The Illustrated Encyclopedia of Dinosaurs.* 1985
—. *The Age of Dinosaurs.* 1985
—. *Dinosaur!* 1991

Paul, Gregory S. *Predatory Dinosaurs of the World.* 1988

Pinna, Giovanni. *The Illustrated Encyclopedia of Fossils.* 1990

Rojdestvensky, A. *Chasse aux dinosaures dans le desert de Gobi.* 1960

Romer, Alfred S. *Vertebrate Paleontology.* 1966

Russell, Dale A. *An Odyssey in Time: The Dinosaurs of North America.* 1989

Stell, R. *Encyclopedia of Paleoherpetology.* Vols. 14 (*Saurischia*) and 15 (*Ornithischia*). 1969–70

Stout, W., and W. Service. *The Dinosaurs.* 1981

Swinton, W. E. *Dinosaurs.* 1970

Tweedie, M. *The World of Dinosaurs.* 1977

Wallace, Joseph, *The Rise and Fall of the Dinosaur.* 1989

Weishampel, David B., Peter Dodson and Halszka Osmolska. *The Dinosauria.* 1990

Wilford, John Noble. *The Riddle of the Dinosaur.* 1985

# MUSEUMS OF THE WORLD

*The only continent without an exhibit of dinosaurs is Antarctica.*

**ARGENTINA**
**La Plata** La Plata Museum

**AUSTRALIA**
NEW SOUTH WALES
**Sydney** Australian Museum

QUEENSLAND
**Fortitude Valley** Queensland Museum

**AUSTRIA**
**Vienna** Natural History Museum

**BELGIUM**
**Brussels** Royal Institute of Natural Sciences

**BRAZIL**
**Rio de Janeiro** National Museum

**CANADA**

ALBERTA
**Calgary** Zoological Gardens
**Drumheller** Tyrell Museum of Paleontology
**Edmonton** Provincial Museum of Alberta
**Patricia** Dinosaur Provincial Park

ONTARIO
**Ottawa** National Museum of Natural Sciences
**Toronto** Royal Ontario Museum

QUEBEC
**Montreal** Redpath Museum, McGill University

**FRANCE**
**Paris** National Museum of Natural History

**GERMANY**
**Berlin** Natural History Museum, Humboldt University
**Frankfurt** Senckenberg Museum
**Munich** Bavarian State Institute for Palaeontology and Historical Geology
**Münster** Geological and Palaeontological Institute, University of Münster
**Stuttgart** State Museum for Natural History
**Tübingen** Institute and Museum of Geology and Palaeontology, University of Tübingen

**GREAT BRITAIN**
**Birmingham** Birmingham Museum
**Cambridge** Museum of Geology, Cambridge University
**Dorchester** Dinosaur Museum
**Edinburgh** Royal Scottish Museum
**Glasgow** Hunterian Museum, University of Glasgow
**Leicester** Leicestershire Museums
**London** British Museum (Natural History) Crystal Palace Park
**Maidstone** Maidstone Museum
**Oxford** University Museum
**Sandown, Isle of Wight** Museum of Geology

**INDIA**
**Calcutta** Geology Museum, Indian Statistical Institute

**ITALY**
**Venice** Municipal Museum of Natural History

**JAPAN**
**Tokyo** National Science Museum

**MEXICO**
**Mexico City** Natural History Museum

**MONGOLIA**
**Ulan Bator** Mongolian Academy of Sciences, Geological Institute

**MOROCCO**
**Rabat** Museum of Earth Sciences

**NIGER**
**Niamey** National Museum of Niger

**PEOPLE'S REPUBLIC OF CHINA**
**Beijing** Beijing Natural History Museum
**Beipei** Beipei Museum

**POLAND**
**Chrozow** Dinosaur Park
**Warsaw** Institute of Palaeobiology

**SOUTH AFRICA**
**Cape Town** South African Museum
**Johannesburg** Bernard Price Institute for Palaeontological Research
**Nelspruit** Sudwala Dinosaur Park

**SPAIN**
**Madrid** Natural Science Museum

**SWEDEN**
**Uppsala** Palaeontological Museum, Uppsala University

**USSR**
**Leningrad** Central Geological and Prospecting Museum
**Moscow** Palaeontological Museum

**UNITED STATES**
ARIZONA
**Flagstaff** Museum of Northern Arizona

CALIFORNIA
**Berkeley** Museum of Paleontology, University of California
**Los Angeles** Los Angeles County Museum of Natural History

COLORADO
**Denver** Denver Museum of Natural History

CONNECTICUT
**New Haven** Peabody Museum of Natural History, Yale University

ILLINOIS
**Chicago** Field Museum of Natural History

MASSACHUSETTS
**Amherst** Pratt Museum of Natural History
**Cambridge** Museum of Comparative Zoology, Harvard University

MICHIGAN
**Ann Arbor** Exhibit Museum, University of Michigan

MONTANA
**Bozeman** Museum of the Rockies, Montana State University

NEW YORK
**Buffalo** Museum of Science
**New York City** American Museum of Natural History

OHIO
**Cleveland** Cleveland Museum of Natural History

PENNSYLVANIA
**Philadelphia** Academy of Natural Sciences
**Pittsburgh** Carnegie Museum of Natural History

TEXAS
**Fort Worth** Museum of Science
**Houston** Museum of Natural Science

UTAH
**Jensen** Dinosaur National Monument
**Provo** Earth Science Museum, Brigham Young University
**Salt Lake City** Utah Museum of Natural History, University of Utah

**Washington, D.C.** National Museum of Natural History

WYOMING
**Laramie** Geological Museum, University of Wyoming

# LIST OF ILLUSTRATIONS

The following abbreviations have been used: *a* above, *b* below, *c* centre, *l* left, *r* right; AMNH=American Museum of Natural History, New York; BN=Bibliothèque Nationale, Paris; MNHN=Muséum National d'Histoire Naturelle, Paris; NMNS=National Museum of Natural Sciences, Ottawa

## COVER

## OPENING

## CHAPTER 1

17 *Pterodactyl* fossil. MNHN

18–9 Mark Hallett, *Australian Dinosaurs*. Painting in *Science Digest*

20–1 John Martin Janyl, *Sea Monsters*. London, 1841. MNHN

21*a* Tuatara (*Sphenodon punctatus*)

21*b* Dale A. Russell and Ron Seguin, dinosauroid reconstruction (detail of head). 1981. NMNS

## CHAPTER 2

22 Zdeněk Burian, *Iguanodon*, in Augusta and Burian, *Prehistoric Animals*, 1956. Library, MNHN

23 G. F. Sternberg working on the skull of *Chasmosaurus belli*, 1914. Photograph. NMNS

24 Antonio Tempesta, *Porco Marino*, from *Collection of Quadrupeds*. Engraving, 1636. BN

25*a* Robert Plot, *The Natural History of Oxford-Shire*, title page. BN

25*b* Antonio Tempesta, *Crocodile and Other Animals*, from *Collection of Quadrupeds*. Engraving, 1636. BN

26*a* Megalosaur vertebrae. MNHN

26–7 Sellier, *Rocks and Cliffs in Normandy*. Engraving in Dicquemare, *Planches d'histoire naturelle*, 1787. Library, MNHN

27 Megalosaur vertebrae. MNHN

28 *Megalosaurus* teeth and jawbone. Drawing in Buckland, 'Notice on the *Megalosaurus* or Great Fossil Lizard of Stonesfield', 1824. Library, MNHN

29*a* A. Demarly, *Iguanodon* and *Megalosaurus* from the Cretaceous period, in Rengade, *La Création naturelle et les êtres vivants*, 1883. BN

29*b* Teeth and jawbones of iguanas and *Iguanodon*, in Mantell, *Memoir on the Fossil Reptiles of the South-East of England*. MNHN

30 Prehistoric animals. Engraving of reconstructions by Benjamin Waterhouse Hawkins in Crystal Palace Park, London

31*a* Gideon Mantell, first reconstruction of *Iguanodon*, drawing. British Museum (Natural History), London

31*b* Richard Owen with *Dinornis maximus*, photograph in *Memoirs on the Extinct Wingless Birds of New Zealand*, 1879. BN

32–3 Zdeněk Burian, *Trachodon* and *Tyrannosaurus*, in Augusta and Burian, *Prehistoric Animals*, 1956. Library, MNHN

34*a* Othniel Charles Marsh, photograph in G. G. Simpson, *Horses*, 1951. Library, MNHN

34–5 Othniel Charles Marsh (back row, centre) and crew equipped for a dig. Photograph

35*a* Edward Drinker Cope, photograph in G. G. Simpson, *Horses*

35*c* Edward Drinker Cope, reconstruction of an amphibious lizard and the horned lizard *Agathamus silvestris*, in H. F. Osborn, *The Life and Letters of*

*E. D. Cope*, 1931. Library, MNHN

36*a* Camp on the Red Deer River, Alberta, 1913. Photograph. NMNS

36*b* *Trachodon* mummy. AMNH

37*a* Fossilized dinosaur skin. AMNH

37*b* Osborn (right) and Brown with *Diplodocus* bones, Aurora, Wyoming. Photograph. AMNH

38*a* *Iguanodons*, drawing. Institut Royal des Sciences Naturelles de Belgique, Brussels

38*b* G. Lavalette, *Iguanodon bernissartensis* in its rock matrix, drawing. Institut Royal des Sciences Naturelles de Belgique, Brussels

39 Becker. Assembling the first skeleton of *Iguanodon bernissartensis* in St. George's Chapel, Brussels, 1884. Painting. Institut Royal des Sciences Naturelles de Belgique, Brussels

40*a* *Protoceratops* skull from the Gobi Desert. MNHN

40*b* Roy Chapman Andrews with two petrified dinosaur eggs found in Central Asia, 1923. Photograph in *L'Illustration*

41 Excavation site, Tibet, 1976

42–3 Jacob Wortman and Walter Granger in a tent, Bone Cabin Camp. Photograph Thomson. AMNH

44*bl* Walter Granger with bones left *in situ*, Bone Cabin Quarry, Wyoming. Photograph Menker. AMNH

44*br* Levi Sternberg wrapping a *Chasmosaurus* skull, Belli River, Alberta, 1914. Photograph. NMNS

45*bl* Hoisting a wrapped *Chasmosaurus* specimen. Photograph. NMNS

45*br* Transporting fossils from the quarry. Photograph. NMNS

## CHAPTER 3

46 Eleanor Kish, *Dromiceiomimus* (detail), painting. NMNS

47 Eleanor Kish, *Dromiceiomimus* (detail), painting. NMNS

48–9 *Ouranosaurus nigeriensis* skeleton from the Ligabue-Taquet expedition, Ténéré Desert, Niger. Museo Civico di Storia Naturale, Venice

48*b* Jean-Guy Michard. Saurischian and ornithischian hipbones. Watercolour

50*l* Assembling *Diplodocus* in the Hall of Palaeontology, MNHN. Photograph in *Le Petit Journal*, 1908

50*r* Femur showing imprint of muscle insertion. MNHN

51*a* *Anatosaurus* femur showing muscle insertion

51*b* Reconstructing a dinosaur skeleton. AMNH

52*a* *Tyrannosaurus* skull. MNHN

52*cl* Teeth of carnivorous dinosaurs. MNHN

52*cr* *Megalosaurus* tooth. MNHN

52*b* *Hadrosaurus* tooth. MNHN

53 *Compsognathus cornallintris* specimen showing stomach contents. MNHN

## PHOTO CREDITS

# ACKNOWLEDGMENTS

The publishers would like to thank Helen Brisson of the National Museum of Natural Sciences in Ottawa and Mr Ligabue of the Museo Civico di Storia Naturale in Venice for their kind assistance with the production of this book. Grateful acknowledgment is made for use of material from the following: Aldiss, Brian W., *Cryptozoic!*, © 1967 by Brian W. Aldiss. Used by permission of Doubleday, a division of Bantam Doubleday Dell Publishing Group, Inc. (p. 121–3). American Museum of Natural History, Special Collections (microfilm) (p. 104–5). Andrews, Roy Chapman, *On the Trail of Ancient Man*, G. P. Putnam's Sons, 1926 (p. 105–12). Doyle, Sir Arthur Conan, *The Lost World*, The Review of Reviews Company, 1912. Reprinted with permission. All Rights Reserved (p. 114–21). Calvin and Hobbes by Bill Watterson. *Something Under the Bed Is Drooling* by Bill Watterson copyright © 1988 by Universal Press Syndicate. All Rights Reserved (p. 127). *Yukon Ho!* by Bill Watterson copyright © 1989 by Universal Press Syndicate. All Rights Reserved (p. 126). The Far Side by Gary Larson. *Beyond the Far Side* by Gary Larson copyright © 1983 by the Chronicle Publishing Company. All Rights Reserved (pp. 124, 125*a*, 125*l*). *In Search of the Far Side* by Gary Larson copyright © 1980, 1983, 1984 by the Chronicle Publishing Company. All Rights Reserved (p. 125*r*).

Jean-Guy Michard
is a palaeontologist specializing in
dinosaurs. After winning the Fondation de la
Vocation prize in 1985, he took part in several
expeditions to Africa and currently oversees
expeditions inside France. He divides his time
between research at the Institute of Palaeontology
of the National Museum of Natural History in Paris
– where he is currently investigating the evolution
and diversification of carnivorous dinosaurs,
including the smallest carnosaur of them all,
Compsognathus – and lecturing to
schoolchildren.

*To my son, Clement. May your eyes never
cease to marvel.*

© Gallimard 1989

English translation © Thames and Hudson Ltd,
London, and Harry N. Abrams, Inc., New York,
1992

Reprinted 1994

Translated by I. Mark Paris

Printed and bound in Italy by
Editoriale Libraria, Trieste